PS
3558
.E4962
L8
1987

THE LUCKY SPOT

A PLAY BY

BETH HENLEY

★

**DRAMATISTS
PLAY SERVICE**
INC.

Dramatists Play Service

ESTABLISHED BY MEMBERS OF THE
DRAMATISTS' GUILD OF THE AUTHORS' LEAGUE OF AMERICA

for the

HANDLING OF THE ACTING RIGHTS
OF MEMBERS' PLAYS

and

THE ENCOURAGEMENT OF THE AMERICAN THEATRE

THE LAST WORD IN MAKE-UP

A Practical Illustrated Handbook

By DR. RUDOLPH LISZT

Revised Edition

A work for all who use make-up on the stage, in the classroom, in the photographer's studio, and TV stations. Compact and easy to understand, it is pre-eminently practical. It is one of the most completely illustrated works issued on this art, containing 44 half-tone photographs (unretouched) and over 80 original drawings by the author, who has been make-up artist for major motion picture studios.

Press Comments

"THE LAST WORD IN MAKE-UP *is the only book on the subject containing a complete, easily followed chart that offers at a glance instructions for the creation of hundreds of parts and characters from A to Z.*"

—FILM DAILY

"*[Dr. Liszt's] book* THE LAST WORD IN MAKE-UP . . . *is required reading in most drama departments. . . .*"

—ORLANDO SENTINEL

One paper volume $6.00

440 PARK AVENUE SOUTH   NEW YORK, N. Y. 10016

Set for the New York production of "The Lucky Spot." Designed by John Lee Beatty.

PHOTO © 1987, BY GERRY GOODSTEIN

THE LUCKY SPOT

A PLAY BY
BETH HENLEY

★

DRAMATISTS
PLAY SERVICE
INC.

© Copyright, 1987, by Beth Henley

CAUTION: Professionals and amateurs are hereby warned that THE LUCKY SPOT is subject to a royalty. It is fully protected under the copyright laws of the United States of America, and of all countries covered by the International Copyright Union (including the Dominion of Canada and the rest of the British Commonwealth), and of all countries covered by the Pan-American Copyright Convention and the Universal Copyright Convention, and of all countries with which the United States has reciprocal copyright relations. All rights, including professional, amateur, motion picture, recitation, lecturing, public reading, radio broadcasting, television, video or sound taping, all other forms of mechanical or electronic reproduction, such as information storage and retrieval systems and photocopying, and the rights of translation into foreign languages, are strictly reserved. Particular emphasis is laid upon the question of readings, permission for which must be secured from the author's agent in writing.

The stage performance rights in THE LUCKY SPOT (other than first class rights) are controlled exclusively by the DRAMATISTS PLAY SERVICE, INC., 440 Park Avenue South, New York, N.Y. 10016. No professional or non-professional performance of the play (excluding first class professional performance) may be given without obtaining in advance the written permission of the DRAMATISTS PLAY SERVICE, INC., and paying the requisite fee.

Inquiries concerning all other rights should be addressed to Gilbert Parker, c/o William Morris Agency, Inc., 1350 Avenue of the Americas, New York, N.Y. 10019.

SPECIAL NOTE

All groups receiving permission to produce THE LUCKY SPOT are required (1) to give credit to the author as sole and exclusive author of the play in all programs distributed in connection with performances of the play and in all instances in which the title of the play appears for purposes of advertising, publicizing or otherwise exploiting the play and/or a production thereof; the name of the author must appear on a separate line, in which no other name appears, immediately beneath the title and in size of type equal to the largest letter used for the title of the play, and (2) to give the following acknowledgement in all programs distributed in connection with performances of the play:

"New York Premiere
by the Manhattan Theatre Club
on April 9, 1987"

SPECIAL NOTE ON MUSIC AND RECORDINGS

For performance of such music and recordings mentioned in this play as are in copyright, the permission of the copyright owners must be obtained; or other music and recordings in the public domain substituted.

SOUND EFFECTS RECORD

The following sound effects record, which may be used in connection with production of this play, can be obtained from Thomas J. Valentino, Inc., 151 West 46th Street, New York, N.Y. 10036.

No. 5041 — Auto sounds

With love to Susan Kingsley and her two kids Roxie and Gar.

THE LUCKY SPOT was presented by Manhattan Theatre Club (Lynne Meadow, Artistic Director; Barry Grove, Managing Director) at City Center Theatre in New York City on April 9, 1987. It was directed by Stephen Tobolowsky; the sets were by John Lee Beatty; the costumes were by Jennifer Von Mayrhauser; the lighting was by Dennis Parichy; the sound was by Scott Lehrer; the production stage manager was Peggy Peterson; and the fight staging was by B. H. Barry. The cast, in order of appearance, was as follows:

CASSIDY SMITH............ Mary Stuart Masterson
TURNIP MOSS........................ Alan Ruck
REED HOOKER........................ Ray Baker
WHITT CARMICHAEL.............. Lanny Flaherty
LACEY ROLLINS.................. Belita Moreno
SUE JACK TILLER HOOKER......... Amy Madigan
SAM.................................. John Wylie

The world premiere of THE LUCKY SPOT was presented by the Williamstown Theatre Festival, Nikos Psacharopolous, Artistic Director.

CHARACTERS

CASSIDY SMITH, 15, works at the Lucky Spot dance hall.
TURNIP MOSS, 20's, works at the Lucky Spot.
REED HOOKER, 40's, owner of the Lucky Spot.
WHITT CARMICHAEL, 30's, a wealthy visitor from New Orleans.
LACEY ROLLINS, 30's, a taxi dancer.
SUE JACK TILLER HOOKER, 30's, Reed Hooker's estranged wife, a former taxi dancer.
SAM, late 60's, a patron of the Lucky Spot.

SETTING

The entire action of the play takes place at the Lucky Spot Dance Hall in Pigeon, Louisiana, a small southern town about sixty miles west of New Orleans. The dance hall is located along the main road at the edge of town.

The dance hall is actually an old Victorian farmhouse. The main room of which has recently been converted into a ballroom with a dancing area, a bar, a jukebox, and a carousel horse that spins. A few tables and a lot of chairs are stacked up together against the wall.

There are four entrances and exits to the ballroom: a swinging door Left that leads to the kitchen; a staircase leading to the upstairs; a front door; and a side door Right, leading to an outdoor area.

The outdoor area consists of an old wood stump and a leafless tree.

TIME

Christmas Eve, 1934.

MUSIC SUGGESTIONS*

ACT I
MUSIC A: "We're In The Money" with Ginger Rogers vocal, 1931.

MUSIC B: Ike "Yowse suh" Hatch and His orchestra's recording of "Some of These Days," London, 1935.

ACT II
MUSIC A: "I Need A Little Sugar In My Bowl," Bessie Smith, vocal, 1931.

MUSIC B: Valaida Snow's trumpet solo on "I Must Have That Man," London, 1937. Repeat the whole song (pg.)

MUSIC C: Fletcher Henderson's "Twelfth Street Rag," Crown Records, 1931. Repeat (pg.)

MUSIC D: Jimmie Noone and Earl Hines' recording of "King Joe," Chicago, 1928.

MUSIC E: Jimmie Noone and Earl Hines' recording of "Sweet Lorraine" — Take 2, Chicago, 1928.

MUSIC F: Coleman Hawkins' recording of "Honeysuckle Rose," London, 1934.

MUSIC G: James Price Johnson, piano solo, "Crying' For The Carolines," New York, 1930.

MUSIC H: Jimmie Noone and Earl Hines' recording of "Sweet Lorraine" — Take 1, Chicago, 1928.

MUSIC I: Louis Armstrong and His Orchestra's recording of "On the Sunny Side of the Street," with Louis Armstrong 100 vocal, Paris, 1934.

---

*See Special Note on copyright page.

THE LUCKY SPOT

ACT I

Cassidy Smith, 15, sits behind the counter writing slowly on a piece of oatmeal carton. She wears a derby hat and loose fitted dull colored garments. Music A plays on the jukebox.*
Turnip Moss enters the outdoor area, dragging a freshly cut pine tree. Turnip, 20's, is a wiry young man with deep watchful eyes.
Turnip hauls the tree in through the side door to the ballroom.

TURNIP. Morning.
CASSIDY. Oh look! Look at this! You're bringing in a tree. We're gonna have a Christmas tree!
TURNIP. Think it's big enough?
CASSIDY. Why it's bigger than me. (*Cassidy comes out from behind the bar. We see that she is about eight months pregnant.*)
TURNIP. Yeah; I guess. Wonder where it oughta go?
CASSIDY. Don't know. Never put a tree inside a room before.
TURNIP. Well, how 'bout . . . how 'bout . . . 'how 'bout . . . How 'bout we put it over here by the staircase? That way people can see it as they're sashaying down the stairs.
CASSIDY. Oh, yeah, that'd be good!
TURNIP. You think it looks good there?
CASSIDY. Uh-uh.
TURNIP. I think it looks good there too. Damn good.
CASSIDY. Yep. You heard anything from Hooker? (*Turnip goes to pour himself the last of the coffee.*)

---

*See Special Note on copyright page.

TURNIP. No. He's been out all night long. Sure hope he struck it lucky.
CASSIDY. Yeah. Hey, Turnip. (*Indicating writing on the oatmeal carton.*) How's that look to you?
TURNIP. (*Reading.*) "Cassidy Smith Hooker." What's this for?
CASSIDY. It's my name. I'm practicing writing it for when I sign the papers.
TURNIP. Sign what papers?
CASSIDY. My marriage papers.
TURNIP. Who're you marrying?
CASSIDY. (*Pointing to the paper.*) Hooker. See there?
TURNIP. What makes you think you're marrying Hooker?
CASSIDY. He tol' me. He give me this yellow piece a rope for a engagement ring.
TURNIP. Let me see that. Hmm. (*Turnip looks at the rope ring then looks back to Cassidy.*) Well, I don't mean this t'hurt your feelings or nothing, Cassidy; but I think he was just kinda — kidding around with ya.
CASSIDY. No, I don't think he was.
TURNIP. Well, thing is Hooker, he — he's already got a wife.
CASSIDY. Yeah, I know. Sue Jack's her name. But I don't think he cares much for her.
TURNIP. Why not?
CASSIDY. Soon as she's released out from Angola State Penitentiary — he's divorcing her and marrying me.
TURNIP. Who told you that?
CASSIDY. He did. He promised me.
TURNIP. I don't believe it.
CASSIDY. Then don't. (*Cassidy gets a broom and starts sweeping up pine needles.*)
TURNIP. Cassidy . . . you think he's in love with you?
CASSIDY. (*Sweeping.*) I didn't say that. I don't care nothing 'bout that. I don't even believe in all that.
TURNIP. Well, when you get married to a person, you're supposed to be in love with the person you're getting married to. I know that much. And people have called me dumb.
CASSIDY. Just look at all these pine needles. It's a damn mess you've made hauling in that ole tree.

TURNIP. You better believe how he was in love with Sue Jack. She's beautiful, and smart, all full of laughing times. Why she was a real lady. Always wore fine lace gloves on her hands so that she could keep her fingertips soft for playing cards.

CASSIDY. Yeah, well I went out this morning and talked to them dancing women out back. Some of 'em used to work with her at the dime a dance halls over in New Orleans. They tol' me she was a broken down wreck. And they put her away for throwing some rich lady over a balcony railing.

TURNIP. That's right — that lady's named Caroline Carmichael. Sue Jack come in a found her lyin' in bed with Hooker and she don't like nobody messing with her man. See, she's very touchy. 'Specially when she drinks. Meanest damn drunk I ever heard of or saw. (*Reed Hooker, mid-40's, enters from the front door. His white shirt is torn and a bloody handkerchief is tied around one of his arms. There is a worn mournful look in his eyes that belies his dashing exuberance.*)

HOOKER. Well, now top of the morning and a Merry Christmas Eve t'the both of ya.

CASSIDY	TURNIP
(*Overlapping*)	(*Overlapping*)
Hooker, you're back!	Did ya win any money?

HOOKER. (*Running on.*) What's this? A Christmas tree? Well, I do love the color green. It's the color of cash!

CASSIDY. What's all this blood?

TURNIP. Do ya like it by the stairway?

HOOKER. Knife wound. No, no, by the window so they can see it from the road.

CASSIDY. Who cut ya? Who done it?

HOOKER. Ah, self-inflicted misfortune.

TURNIP. (*As if this were obvious.*) Oh sure, from the road. They gotta see it from the road.

CASSIDY. Well, I'll get ya some cobwebs from out in the barn t'help staunch the bleeding. (*Hooker picks up Cassidy and twirls her around in his arms.*)

HOOKER. Now aren't you the sweetest girl in the whole wide world and her with her six little toes.

CASSIDY. Don't talk about my toes.

HOOKER. She's got the prettiest little toes.

TURNIP. Six all on one foot. I've seen 'em.
CASSIDY. I said stop talking about my toes less you want me to slice your eyes out — I don't like to hear nothing about that. You're just making your fun outta me.
HOOKER. No, no, I ain't making my fun outta you. Why, I been out all night long bucking the tiger just to bring you back a Christmas gift.
CASSIDY. A Christmas gift for me?! (*Hooker gets a jug of whiskey, from behind the counter, and throughout the following downs a couple of belts.*)
TURNIP. I bet she's never had a Christmas gift.
CASSIDY. I have, too.
TURNIP. Mr. Pete never gave her anything but a cat-o'-nine tails from what I hear.
CASSIDY. My mama used t'give us an orange and a peppermint candy every Christmas morning.
TURNIP. Your mama's been dead almost ten years.
CASSIDY. I remember it though. (*To Hooker.*) So what'd ya bring t'me?
HOOKER. Well, Saucer Eyes, I was gonna bring ya a solid gold hat with red ostrich plumes, and Turnip, I was gonna bring you a pocket full of Mexican jumping beans. Unfortunately, I got hooked up in a godless card game. Lost my luck late. Came outta there with nothing but the mist of the morning dew.
CASSIDY. Well, what in the world was I gonna do with another hat? I already got this one.
HOOKER. Ah, six months from now, we'll be eating outta hats. Soon as we get the Lucky Spot Dance Hall rolling.
TURNIP. Yeah, well, I sure hope the place goes over big tonight 'cause we're flat broke around here.
HOOKER. Hey, look, it's Christmas Eve. People are so lonely out there you can smell it rotting on 'em. Here at the Lucky Spot we'll be selling hot music, fine dancing and sweet solace of kindhearted women.
CASSIDY. I can't wait to see it with all the lights and music and the women in their long shiny gowns dancing with all the lonely souls.
HOOKER. We're gonna make a fortune.

TURNIP. I just hope they don't tear down the doors fighting t'get in.
CASSIDY. It'll be more like a dream than something real.
HOOKER. Well, now enough gold bricking. Let's get up our Christmas tree. We got any coffee left?
CASSIDY. I'll make a new pot. And I'll fix ya some breakfast.
HOOKER. Fine, fine, but do me a favor and don't put that greasy gravy all over everything on the plate.
CASSIDY. I won't. I'll make it real good this time. Real good. I promise.
HOOKER. Yeah. (*Cassidy exits to the kitchen. Throughout the following Hooker and Turnip make a wooden Christmas tree stand and put the tree into it.*) She's not a bad kid but I swear to God she is the worst damn cook I ever knew.
TURNIP. Well, what can you expect? You won her in a poker game.
HOOKER. Yeah, well maybe I should have taken the chestnut mare.
TURNIP. Why didn't ya?
HOOKER. Oh, you know . . . her face.
TURNIP. What about it?
HOOKER. That woebegone countenance. I don't know. Anyway, it's done. Come on and help me with this tree.
TURNIP. Hooker?
HOOKER. Huh?
TURNIP. It's about Cassidy. I think she's suffering from some sort of grand delusion.
HOOKER. Hold this here. Hold it tight now.
TURNIP. See, cause she is claiming you told her you'd marry her.
HOOKER. Oh yeah?
TURNIP. Yeah, she seems to be counting on it.
HOOKER. Look, I'm already married. Remember? To the ditch digger's daughter.
TURNIP. Yeah, well, Cassidy said you were gonna divorce Sue Jack and marry her. She claims you promised her.
HOOKER. Christ, I never promised her. (*A beat.*) Maybe I intimated something about the faint possibility.

TURNIP. Why would ya do a thing like that?
HOOKER. I don't know, Turnip. Maybe I just got fed up with the way she kept rolling herself down the staircase and eating boxes of match heads and banging at her belly with a two-by-four.
TURNIP. Oh, ya mean she didn't want t'have no kid.
HOOKER. I don't think she did, no. (*Hooker gets a banner from behind the counter.*) Here, let's get up the sign.
TURNIP. (*A beat.*) Gosh, so what're ya gonna do about Sue Jack when she gets out of prison? Would you divorce her for real?
HOOKER. God, no. I'd just shoot the bitch on sight.
TURNIP. Yeah, well, yep. But you ain't still mad at her about it all?
HOOKER. The hell I'm not.
TURNIP. But she loved him same as you. After it happened she got all torn up inside.
HOOKER. Bullshit! She was glad to be rid of both of us. The night after they laid my kid in the ground she went out to a cockfight in a red tassled dress and squandered away her wedding ring. She went on boozing and brawling and lavishing away everything decent we ever had together. Don't ever mention her to me! Don't ever mention her to me!
TURNIP. Okay, okay. I won't; I won't! So, ah, what's gonna happen with Cassidy, I mean concerning the predicament ya got her in.
HOOKER. Look, she'll have the kid. The Lucky Spot'll be in full swing. I'll send her off to some respectable school, let 'em teach her how t'cook. She'll find a nice guy — that'll be that.
TURNIP. (*A beat.*) What about your baby?
HOOKER. I'll just hang on to him.
TURNIP. How do you know she won't want it?
HOOKER. The sign's not even. Your side's too low.
TURNIP. So how're ya gonna tell Cassidy ya ain't marrying her? How're ya gonna spring it on her?
HOOKER. Stop dogging me. I'll spring it on her. I'll spring it on her.
TURNIP. I mean, look at the condition ya got her in. I wouldn't know what the hell t'tell her by now.

HOOKER. Goddamnit, Turnip! Now your side's too high. Bring it down.

TURNIP. I wonder if I'll ever have a girlfriend. My brothers told me I'd never have a girlfriend as long as I had the name Turnip. But I didn't know how to change my name 'cause folks was always calling me by it.

HOOKER. (*Looking up at the sign.*) I reckon that'll do.

TURNIP. I just wish I wasn't plaqued by self-doubt. But I'm afraid of . . . I don't know what, but I bet it's something. (*Cassidy re-enters from the kitchen. She carries a tray with a breakfast plate, silverware, cup and saucer and coffee pot.*)

CASSIDY. Oh, look, ya got up the tree! And look at that. (*She points to the banner and tries to read it as she makes cowboy coffee.*) Let's see. "Well . . . welcome. Welcome to . . . "

TURNIP. (*Reading easily.*) "Welcome to the Grand Opening, Lucky Spot Dance Hall."

HOOKER. (*To imaginary guest.*) Welcome, welcome, welcome.

TURNIP. Yes, sirree, welcome one and all.

CASSIDY. Hooker.

HOOKER. Huh?

CASSIDY. I need to talk to you on a matter. It's kinda . . . pressing. (*Hooker and Turnip exchange a meaningful glance.*)

HOOKER. Yeah, we're gonna have some fun tonight!

CASSIDY. Here's your breakfast for ya.

HOOKER. Thanks. (*Hooker takes the plate, looks at it and smirks derogatorily, then shakes his head to Turnip.*)

CASSIDY. It look bad to you?

HOOKER. It looks like it always looks when you cook breakfast.

CASSIDY. I'll take it back.

HOOKER. No, no. I'll eat it. (*Cassidy reaches for the plate to take it and Hooker notices her hand.*) Don't you ever wash your hands?

CASSIDY. . . . Sure.

HOOKER. Well, you could plant a vegetable garden underneath those fingernails. Don't you ever clean them?

CASSIDY. Yeah, I just . . . when I'm working, well the

dirt gets stuck there and I can't never get it out.
HOOKER. Try scraping it with a hairpin.
CASSIDY. I ain't got no hairpins.
HOOKER. Then use a nail or a fork or something, for Christ sake!
CASSIDY. (*Picking up Hooker's fork.*) Okay.
HOOKER. Not my fork, God damn it! Look, I don't mean to harp on you about this or anything. We're pals, right? Come on. I'll try and eat some of this slop. I'm sure it isn't too horrible. Jesus Christ, you're not gonna start t'cry just 'cause I tell you you should wash your filthy hands once a goddamn century?!
CASSIDY. No, I'll . . . I'll go wash 'em. I'm just needing to talk to you, that's all. I'll wash up and come on back. (*Cassidy exits up the stairs. Hooker turns to Turnip.*)
HOOKER. Jesus. Women. They're all alike. Them girls out back. You stay ten miles clear of any whiff of 'em — that's my best advice. (*Whitt Carmichael, 30's, enters through the front door. He is a tall man with an imposing elegance. He wears an expensive but understated suit and carries an alligator attache case.*)
TURNIP. Howdy.
CARMICHAEL. Reed Hooker?
HOOKER. What can I do for you?
CARMICHAEL. Well now, I'd like to discuss with you briefly my involvement in the ownership of this property. (*Hooker stares at Carmichael, poker-faced.*) The story is that you won it off my cousin, Davenport Fletcher, in a five-day card game down on the Gulf Coast.
HOOKER. Yes, well, that's how that story goes.
CARMICHAEL. This was my aunt's estate and she did leave it to Davenport. Now, the only problem I perceive is my cousin's three hundred and fifty-five dollar debt to me that he used this house as collateral against. Right here's a copy of the papers alerting you of the situation. (*Carmichael hands Hooker a document. Hooker takes it.*) Of course, I can see you've made some . . . improvements.
HOOKER. Yeah, well, they're a lot of initial expenses you accrue when starting out a new business. And there's always

a bit of difficulty with handing out the ready cash; so as I'm sure you can imagine, your request for payment in full is difficult for me at this time. However, if you're a hunch bettor, I believe I could finagle you some points in the Lucky Spot that could triple your money for you in about a year's time.

CARMICHAEL. Then you honestly think this place is going to make money?

HOOKER. I'm afraid it's bound for glory. The Lucky Spot will be the first genuine taxi dance hall set in an isolated rural area. The glamour, magic and music of the city sporting life will now be available to the simple country folk who secretly ache for such dazzling companionship on so many of these lonely moonless nights.

TURNIP. Yeah, we got the flyers up all over town. Everyone's talking the place up big.

HOOKER. Yes, all of our dance teachers have been hired directly out of New Orleans. They split their take fifty-fifty with the hall. We also get all of the door and, of course, the extras.

TURNIP. (*Holding up a hanger of old neckties.*) Yeah, like these neckties you can rent for ten cents at the door in case, say, you forgot your own necktie . . . or in case, say, you never had no neckties at all.

HOOKER. Of course, the real saving grace, economically speaking, is the jukebox. Isn't she a beauty? See, we won't have to pay a nickel to any local musicians for playing their lousy marshmallow music. Why, we've got twenty-six of the newest tunes, played by the hottest bands, right at our fingertips. So what d'ya say, pal? Are you a hunch bettor?

CARMICHAEL. As a matter of fact, Mr. Hooker, I am somewhat of a gambler and I believe I'm going to have a bet against this depressing little monkey hop and the foolhearted ex-rumrunner who doesn't have a Chinaman's chance of making a business out a racket.

HOOKER. Well, now, would anybody care to add to that; or maybe subtract?

CARMICHAEL. I'll make it simple: give me the cash or I close down the hall.

HOOKER. How long do I have?

CARMICHAEL. I believe that order the sheriff signed allows you 'till January one. Time's almost up.

HOOKER. You're a real sport. But I'm too many miles down the road t'turn back now. (*Hooker produces a deck of cards.*) Here let's cut for it. Double or nothing.

CARMICHAEL. Afraid not.

HOOKER. (*With a forced grin.*) Look . . . it's Christmas.

CARMICHAEL. Well, I'm not Santa Claus. (*Cassidy comes running down the stairs excitedly. She carries a comb.*)

CASSIDY. (*About her fingernails.*) Look! Look here, I scraped out every scrap of dirt from underneath there using the teeth on this here comb.

HOOKER. Ah, great work.

CASSIDY. Thanks. (*Extending her spotless hand to Carmichael.*) Hi, Mister!

TURNIP. This man's trying t'close down the Lucky Spot. Says Hooker owes him a lot a money.

CASSIDY. Well then, Hooker'll just have t'have himself another lucky streak. Just like he did that time down in Gulfport when he won me and this place and the Chevy motor car.

CARMICHAEL. All that. Well now, Mr. Hooker, you do seem to be quite a lucky man. But then I guess you did pick up a few gambling tips from your very talented wife.

CASSIDY. How d'you know his wife?

HOOKER. What d'ya know about her?

CARMICHAEL. Hmm. Well. I've played cards with her on occasion. And then there was a time when I was bringing my sister, Caroline Carmichael, back and forth from the hospital every day to testify against Mrs. Hooker at her trial.

HOOKER. Good Christ, he's Caroline Carmichael's brother!

TURNIP. No wonder he hates your damn guts.

HOOKER. Yeah, well, he can hate my guts as much as he wants to, but it wasn't me who shoved Caroline over that goddamn balcony railing! Sue Jack did it all on her own. (*To Carmichael.*) So you stop harassing us 'cause of that no good wife of mine?! God, I'd love t'break her rotten neck and shut

her up for good!
CARMICHAEL. Lucky you didn't shut her up before you mastered all of her card playing pointers.
HOOKER. What pointers do you mean?
CARMICHAEL. Your wife was an expert card sharp; had great hands, knew all about shaved cards, hold outs . . . ringing in a cold deck.
HOOKER. What are you inferring?
CARMICHAEL. I'm not inferring.
HOOKER. Look, like you say, Sue Jack had the hands. You gotta have the hands. I never did. Nah, there's only one thing I learned from Sue Jack that ever did me any good.
CARMICHAEL. Now what would that be?
HOOKER. A simple rule of thumb: whoever throws the first punch in a fist fight has a twenty-to-one shot at aceing the match. (*The two men stare at each other.*)
CARMICHAEL. Is that a fact? (*Hooker shrugs his shoulders and turns.*)
HOOKER. Seems t'be. Hey! (*Hooker turns back and clobbers Carmichael in the jaw. Carmichael falls to the floor.*) Sorry I pasted him, but he was becoming insufferable.
CARMICHAEL. You're gonna regret this. Believe me, you're gonna regret this a lot. I'm calling in the Sheriff.
HOOKER. Hey, Turnip, help the man outa here. (*Turnip pulls Carmichael to his feet and ushers him towards the door.*)
CARMICHAEL. You're outta here. You're through. Pack your goddamn bags! You're finished! (*Hooker yells after them as Turnip and Carmichael exit out the front door.*)
HOOKER. (*Overlapping.*) Relax, Carmichael. I'll have that money for ya by January one! No damn problem with the Lucky Spot opening. No damn problem!
TURNIP. (*Offstage*) No damn problem!
HOOKER. Jesus!
CASSIDY. Looks like you got that man pretty riled up.
HOOKER. Looks like it.
CASSIDY. You reckon he's gonna get us kicked outta here for good?
HOOKER. Look, the Lucky Spot Dance Hall opens at 8 p.m. tonight; by 9:15 we'll be strolling on Easy Street; by January

one, you'll be dancing in satin red shoes. Every day's gonna be like a goddamn holiday in Paris, France! Now do ya have that straight?
CASSIDY. Uh huh.
HOOKER. Well, good. 'Cause I'm sure as hell not standing here telling ya all this crap just t'get your rotten hopes up for nothing.
CASSIDY. No, I — I sure I don't wanna get my rotten hopes up for nothing. 'Cause my hopes . . . well, sometimes, when they get way, way up there, I don't even know how t'get 'em back down without dying or not living or breathing or exploding. I don't know why. Sometimes.
HOOKER. Yeah. Sure. Well, I would never want t'get your hopes up for nothing.
CASSIDY. Thanks. I appreciate it. (*They look at the floor for a moment.*) Hooker?
HOOKER. Yeah?
CASSIDY. I got this thing for you. (*Cassidy takes a dirty worn piece of paper out of her pocket.*)
HOOKER. What is it?
CASSIDY. Just a card. A birthday message.
HOOKER. Well, my birthday was way back in the damn summer.
CASSIDY. I know. I been carrying the card around since then.
HOOKER. Uh-huh.
CASSIDY. But I just never could find the right time t' . . . give it to ya.
HOOKER. Oh. (*Cassidy hands out the card then withdraws it.*)
CASSIDY. Nah, maybe I should wait and go on and give it to you some other time.
HOOKER. Well, I may as well look at the thing.
CASSIDY. There's nothing particular about it.
HOOKER. Okay, if you don't want me t'have it . . .
CASSIDY. No, no. Go on. Here. It's for you. (*She hands him the card.*)
HOOKER. (*Hooker unfolds the paper and reads the message aloud.*) "To Reed Hooker. Happy Birthday. From Cassidy Smith." The "K"'s backwards. (*He hands the paper back to her.*)

CASSIDY. Well . . . okay.
HOOKER. I gotta go wash up. (*Hooker starts up the stairs.*)
CASSIDY. I'll, ah, I'll run iron ya your clean shirt. (*Hooker exits up the stairs. Cassidy exits out the kitchen door carrying the breakfast tray. Lacy Rollins, a shortish woman in her 30's, with peroxided hair and heavy rouge, appears outside dressed in a frilly, tattered robe and high heels. She stumbles across the yard and moves into the dance hall through the side door. She looks around, sees the room is deserted, spots the coffee pot and starts looking for a cup. Turnip walks in through the front door. He eyes her nervously.*)
TURNIP. Hi.
LACEY. (*Startled.*) I was just coming in from out back t'hunt me some coffee. I need t'have coffee every morning. Otherwise, my heart just won't start pumping and it's likely I'll drop into a dead heap right here on this floor.
TURNIP. Well there's the coffee pot right there.
LACEY. I see it, but I'm gonna need me a cup. Do you know where there's a cup? Or even a bowl? I don't mind drinking outta bowls. I don't have t'be prissy. (*Turnip finds a cup.*)
TURNIP. Here, use this.
LACEY. Thanks. I don't guess there's any sugar?
TURNIP. No.
LACEY. Oh, well. It's just I love sugar. You can't ruin sugar. I wish I could put it on every morsel I ever ate. Wouldn't it be wonderful poured all over your scrambled eggs, and your sausages and your grits?
TURNIP. I never thought t'give it a try. (*Lacey moves around the room.*)
LACEY. Well, I've thought t'give it a try. I've thought and thought and thought and — (*Lacey trips on her robe and falls to the floor. On the verge of tears.*) Oh dear. Look here, I've tripped again. I'm always falling down. I've got very weak ankles. My ankle bones are practically the smallest bones in my body. It's a condition that I've had since early birth. (*Starting to cry.*) Oh Lord. I'm sorry if I seem t'be falling apart. My goodness, it's only Christmas Eve and already I'm emotional.
TURNIP. Is something wrong?
LACEY. Well, where am I supposed to go? What am I sup-

posed to do? Tomorrow's Christmas Day, and I'm sure no one's even thought to get me a present. I'm stuck out here in this backwoods without a nickel in my stocking—
TURNIP. What're you talking about? You'll be dancing here at the Lucky Spot tonight. You'll clear some jack. (*Hooker comes down the stairs without wearing a shirt.*)
HOOKER. Hey, Cassidy, where's the clean shirt? (*Noticing Lacey and Turnip*) Oh, good morning, Lacey, right? Hope you girls had a good night's sleep. Ya'll all gotta look real beautiful for tonight.
LACEY. Don't you know?
HOOKER. Know what?
LACEY. The other girls have all gone. They're all catching the train back t'New Orleans. And not a stinking one of 'em would lend me the fare. They don't like me. I'm unpopular everywhere I go. (*Cassidy enters from the kitchen with a clean shirt.*)
HOOKER. What're you saying? The girls aren't out back in the bungalows? (*Turnip runs out to check the bungalows.*)
LACEY. Bungalows? He calls those bungalows! Why, everyone of us recognized them to be authentic slave quarters. I don't care what fancy colors you paint them.
HOOKER. Look, what's happening here? (*Turnip enters.*)
TURNIP. They're gone alright.
HOOKER. Why'd everyone go?
LACEY. They all heard she was coming back.
HOOKER. Who?
LACEY. Your wife, Sue Jack. They're all scared t'death of her—think she's dangerous.
HOOKER. For Christ sake, she's in prison. She's no more coming here than Santa Claus.
LACEY. Well, the kid in the derby hat seems to be differently informed.
HOOKER. (*To Cassidy.*) What do you know about Sue Jack coming here? (*Hooker takes the shirt from Cassidy and starts to put it on.*)
CASSIDY. Well, it's just I been keeping in check with the lady over at Angola Penitentiary . . .
HOOKER. You what?
CASSIDY. Yeah. And she tells me there's a special order

releasing some prisoners out early for Christmas time and Sue Jack's one of 'em.
HOOKER. Well, she sure as shit's not coming here for Christmas!
CASSIDY. Yeah, she is. 'Cause I told 'em where we was.
TURNIP. Oh Lord!
CASSIDY. And we wanted her to come on out here.
HOOKER. I oughta bust you, Cassidy. I oughta bust you good! Is this any of your goddamn business?! (*To Lacey.*) How long ago did the girls leave here for the train depot?
LACEY. I don't know. A while, I guess.
HOOKER. I gotta drive over there and stop them. (*To Turnip who echoes his words.*) Look, if she . . . if she comes here . . . (*Hooker shoves Cassidy, who is trying to stop him, into the door.*) God damn it! . . . you tell her to get out and stay out. She's not welcome ever.
CASSIDY. But you don't understand! She's gotta be here t'get her divorce so you can oblige your marriage t'me. Please. Then she can go away forever! (*Hooker pulls Cassidy up by her hair.*)
HOOKER. Look, I don't want you getting involved with that woman. Stay clear of her! You understand me? Huh?!
CASSIDY. Uh-huh. (*He lets her go.*)
HOOKER. Good. (*Hooker storms out the front door.*)
CASSIDY. He pulled my hair. He never done that before. He never shouted at me like that. I thought he was different, but he's just the same! Oooh! I hate him! I hate him! He's mean and awful! And I hate him forever!
TURNIP. Well, you should never have taken it on your own t'stick your nose in like you did, calling up the prison, telling them t'send Sue Jack here.
CASSIDY. (*Turning on him.*) Yeah, well, how else is she gonna get her divorce so I can get my marriage? Huh? Did you ever think of that?! See, 'cause he's just got to marry me soon. Otherwise, this thing will be born out a bastard. And everyone in the world will look down on it and it won't have no excuses at all. (*Breaking into tears of raging fury.*) Oh, he promised me he'd marry me. He promised! He wouldn't break his promise, would he? Oh, promise me, he wouldn't!! Promise me!!!

TURNIP. Sure, I promise. I promise. Just don't cry so much.
LACEY. That's right, sugar, all that crying's gonna use up your face. And you've only got this one little face t'get by on for your whole life long. Ya gotta use it up sparingly. (*Turnip gets a bucket of red berries and brings it over to Cassidy.*)
TURNIP. Hey, you wanna start stringing up these berries? We gotta decorate the tree.
CASSIDY. We gonna string these berries then put 'em up on the tree?
TURNIP. Yeah.
CASSIDY. That'll look good.
TURNIP. And there's popcorn. I'll go make the popcorn. We'll string that up, too.
CASSIDY. Okay. (*Turnip exits to the kitchen. Cassidy takes a needle and thread out of her pocket and starts stringing the berries. Lacey watches Cassidy, who is contentedly stringing berries.*)
LACEY. May I help?
CASSIDY. Okay. I got one more needle. (*Cassidy goes to get a needle and thread.*) Tell me.
LACEY. What?
CASSIDY. You reckon Hooker's gonna be able t'bring them dancing ladies back here for tonight?
LACEY. Well, I hope so. Otherwise, my life is simply at a complete loss for direction.
CASSIDY. I should never of spoken nothing about her coming back. I sure didn't guess it'd run 'em all off like that.
LACEY. Oh, those girls are all being horrible, silly, scaredy cats. Why, back when she was dancing in New Orleans, everyone of 'em would of died to be just like her.
CASSIDY. They would of?
LACEY. Sure. Sue Jack Tiller was top girl at the Glitter Dance Palace. She was the most beautiful, the finest dancer, the funniest wit. She made a hobby of collecting diamond engagement rings. She was always fishing guys for silk gowns and mink furs. Why, she possessed this one floor-length white mink coat that all the girls stood dripping with envy over. 'Course it didn't bother me a lick as I've never had the slightest affection for rodents. Pass the berries. (*Cassidy*

passes the bucket of berries to Lacey.)
CASSIDY. Here.
LACEY. None of us could ever fathom why she hauled off and married an insane rumrunner like Reed Hooker. Oh not that he wasn't well-to-do. Prohibition was a very flush time for the rumrunners. Still she could have had anyone. After all she possessed a great many assets.
CASSIDY. Like what?
LACEY. Well now, her greatest asset, in my opinion, was her ability to hold a prolonged conversation with a man. My auntie always told me, if a man would hold a conversation with a woman, well, she was special. She had more than his grudging physical desire — she had his admiration and respectability.
CASSIDY. Well, me, I — I've talked to men. I say things t' 'em and mostly they talk right back.
LACEY. That's different, sugar. What I'm talking about is real conversation. Not things such as "Hi, cutie," or "Hot night," or "Where's my clean shirt?" See, a real conversation would be dealing in topics with much more depth and importance.
CASSIDY. Like what? What would be a real conversation?
LACEY. Hmm. It's hard t'say exactly. But more along the lines of a discussion as to how the sun is really a star and it's made up out of balls of burning fire and once there was an ice age and everything got frozen and died in the cold but then things began to thaw out and the sun came back out and people could start to living again but the dinosaurs were gone forever because they had become . . . extinct.
CASSIDY. Gosh. Well. I'd be confused speaking in a conversation like that.
LACEY. Sure. Most girls would be. Or say, for instance, one might have a conversation discussing deep, frightening things about living and dying that most people would never even mention because they're too stupid t' think 'em up in the first place.
CASSIDY. Like what deep frightening things 'bout living and dying?
LACEY. Oh . . . I don't know exactly. Just a very compli-

cated sort of conversation. I don't get t'practice conversation that much. Most fellows won't pay any attention to me unless I'm being perky. But her . . . they'd have endless conversation with her.
CASSIDY. Still all an' all, I bet she's not one whit better'n me.
LACEY. Well . . . you're a good deal younger than she is. You've got the bloom of youth.
CASSIDY. Yeah; I hope.
LACEY. Does Hooker . . . does he ever tell you he loves you?
CASSIDY. (*Factually.*) Oh no. No person ever told me that. But one night, not long ago, I — I dreamed some furry animal said it loved me, but I don't remember what kind it was.
LACEY. Well, even though I've never really known it, I do believe in love. I don't think I could go on living if I didn't. Unfortunately, I've got a way of making any fellow I'm with so mad he'll haul off and hit me. The last one, he tried t'drowned me in the bathtub. Since then, it's been hard t'let myself trust a man. But I still keep trying. I still believe in love. (*Sue Jack Tiller Hooker, 30's, enters through the front door. She has the jarring presence of a ravaged beauty. She is tall and thin and wears a hand-me-down dress, a thin wool coat and flat ugly shoes. She carries a large handbag.*)
SUE JACK. Hi.
CASSIDY. Hi.
SUE JACK. Is this a dance hall?
CASSIDY. It is.
SUE JACK. Y'all opening tonight?
CASSIDY. We is.
SUE JACK. Oh. Well, good. Good. I — um, is Reed Hooker, is he around here anywhere?
CASSIDY. He's gone out.
SUE JACK. Oh. Well, how long do you think he'll be gone?
CASSIDY. Don't know. What d'ya want with him?
SUE JACK. Well . . . I'm his wife, Sue Jack Hooker . . . I've been away . . . awhile.
CASSIDY. Yeah. Yeah, I heard about you. But you don't look the same as I thought.
SUE JACK. No?

CASSIDY. Uh-huh.
SUE JACK. Um.
LACEY. Oh, hello. I'm sure you don't remember me but I worked at the Green Torch Dance Hall years ago when you were at the Glitter Palace down in New Orleans. My name's Lacey Rollins.
SUE JACK. Oh yeah, I remember you. You did cartwheels.
LACEY. Right. She's right.
SUE JACK. But your hair was much darker back then — It was jet black, almost a blue-black.
LACEY. Why, I'm flabbergasted! Who'd ever have thought you'd remember me? Tell me. Don't you think this new color is much more flattering? Doesn't it give me a much more perky look?
SUE JACK. Well, you were always very . . . perky. But I do, ah, like it a lot.
LACEY. Why, thanks, sugar. And your hair, it's all done . . . well, just completely differently.
SUE JACK. That's right. It's all different now. (*Turnip enters with the popcorn.*)
TURNIP. Well, here's the popcorn.
SUE JACK. Turnip.
TURNIP. Sue Jack?
SUE JACK. Yeah, its me.
TURNIP. Gosh, you look — I mean, your face —
SUE JACK. I know, it looks like forty miles of bad road, all of it rained on. Well, hell, 'least I made it through three years at Angola, that's something.
TURNIP. Oh, sure.
LACEY. Sure.
TURNIP. Boy, I'm glad they set ya free when they did.
SUE JACK. Yeah, I got lucky. They decided to let some of us out early for Christmas. Probably so they could save on turkey dinners.
TURNIP. Well, gosh. Gosh, what was it like stuck in prison? Did y'all have any fun at all? I mean, what did they do on your birthday?
SUE JACK. Well . . . nothing.
TURNIP. Oh.
SUE JACK. Yeah. Nothing special. Just, you know, the same.

TURNIP. What's that like? The same?
SUE JACK. Oh, I can't really afford t'think about all that right now. I wanna try and make a good impression on Reed when he gets here. Tell me, do I really look plain ugly?
LACEY. No!
TURNIP. No it's just . . . different.
LACEY. Different. (*Echoing Turnip.*)
TURNIP. I mean, from before. You don't — got on your gloves. But other than that . . . well, ya don't look ugly.
SUE JACK. Then will ya do me a favor?
TURNIP. What?
SUE JACK. Stop looking at me like that. You're starting t'get me scared.
TURNIP. What? No, there's nothing t'be scared for.
SUE JACK. I know. It's just I gotta see Reed. I haven't seen him in so long. And I'm standing here in these hand-me-down rags, with my hair all cropped off looking like something a cat dragged in.
TURNIP. You look okay.
SUE JACK. Thanks, I'm sorry. I'm just so jumpy today. I swear if somebody said boo t'me I'd cry.
TURNIP. Ain't nobody gonna say boo to ya.
SUE JACK. Sure. I'll be okay. I mean, I was just so surprised that he called for me.
TURNIP. Who called for you?
SUE JACK. Reed. He — he never visited me the whole time, and I thought I'd lost him for sure and here, outta the blue, he calls and leaves a message telling me t'come here for Christmas.
TURNIP. Oh . . . gosh.
SUE JACK. I've got all this hope welling up in me again. I swear my heart's spinning inside me like a runaway top.
TURNIP. Yeah, well, I don't know what t'say here. Umm. Here's the popcorn, Cassidy, if ya wanna start stringing it up.
CASSIDY. Thanks.
SUE JACK. This is a beautiful jukebox. Prettiest one I've ever seen.
TURNIP. It's Hooker's pride and joy. Says it's got all his favorite tunes on it.

SUE JACK. All these tunes are new. I don't recognize any of them.
CASSIDY. Look, there's some things of yours ya might be wanting.
SUE JACK. What things?
CASSIDY. Just belongings. I found 'em in one of the drawers in Hooker's trunk. I put 'em in a box for ya.
SUE JACK. Well, thanks.
CASSIDY. I'll go up and get 'em for ya. Ya might be needing 'em on your travels.
SUE JACK. Alright.
LACEY. (*To Turnip.*) Hey, what was it she called you?
TURNIP. Huh?
LACEY. Was it Turnip? Did she call you "Turnip"?
TURNIP. I guess.
LACEY. Turnip. That's hilarious. Whatever does it stand for?
TURNIP. Just stands for Turnip.
LACEY. But what's it short for?
TURNIP. My name, I guess.
LACEY. Well, what's your name?
TURNIP. . . . Turnip.
LACEY. Oh.
TURNIP. . . . Yeah. (*Whitt Carmichael enters through the front door. He doesn't notice Sue Jack who is seated in the window seat.*)
CARMICHAEL. Hello. Is Hooker here?
TURNIP. No.
CARMICHAEL. Look, I just found out that all of your Gold Coast hostesses have run out in fear of the imminent arrival of Hooker's outlaw wife.
SUE JACK. Why, hello, Whitt.
CARMICHAEL. Sue Jack . . . Good Lord — I hardly recognized you.
SUE JACK. Yes, well, I guess I look kind of different without a frame around me.
CARMICHAEL. Well, well, so the never-miss girl has really returned. Tell me, how are those silk hands of yours? She had the prettiest hands. They never let her down.

SUE JACK. 'Least not to your level, anyway.
CARMICHAEL. You got close though. Back on Esplanade Avenue. You got awfully close. Let me see those hands.
SUE JACK. Oh, it's amazing what three years of raising hogs and picking cotton can do to a pair of hands. Feel for yourself. (*Sue Jack reaches up to rub her calloused fingertips across Carmichael's face. He pulls away.*) Oh Whitt, what's the matter? Don't you wanna see if I lost my touch?
CARMICHAEL. Look . . . I didn't come here to dwell on your hard luck or your felony conviction . . . I have a business proposition to discuss with your husband. (*Cassidy comes walking down the staircase carrying a cardboard box.*)
SUE JACK. Tell me. Reed and I are partners.
CARMICHAEL. Well, in the light of the fact that your dancers have departed, I feel it is now painfully apparent that Hooker will not be able to settle his three hundred and fifty-five dollar debt to me by January first. So, as a matter of convenience, I'd appreciate him signing this property over to me straight away. (*Carmichael hands a paper to Sue Jack. As she looks it over.*) Otherwise, I intend to inform all the people in town Hooker owes money to the distressing news that y'all are opening up your taxi dance hall with absolutely no taxi dancers. Believe me, it could make some of them rubes very, very angry.
SUE JACK. (*Handing the paper back to Turnip.*) I don't know where you get your information, Whitt, but someone just about pulled your leg completely off. Why, our only concern is that there will be so many beautiful ladies dancing here this evening that everyone strolling down this road will be made mindlessly drunk inhaling the intoxicating smell of all the sweet perfumes.
CARMICHAEL. Ah, Sue Jack, I do love it when you wax poetic but I saw all of your charity girls pulling out on this morning's train. They claimed they were escaping your villainous presence.
SUE JACK. That's pure sour grapes. They're just distressed because we rejected them for the dance hall. You see, we only want the creme de le creme working at the Lucky Spot. (*Lacey smiles broadly.*) Come by tonight and see for yourself if you don't believe me.

CARMICHAEL. Don't worry, I'll be back. And so will a lot of other folks who have debts to settle.
SUE JACK. Wonderful. We need some big-time spenders. So long now. Merry Christmas.
CARMICHAEL. And a Merry Christmas to you, Miss Sue.
LACEY. Please do come back. (*Carmichael exits out the front door.*)
SUE JACK. My God. Have all the dancers really gone?
LACEY. I'm afraid so. I'm the only one left.
SUE JACK. I can't believe people think I'm so horrible. I mean, maybe back when I drank I was something of a hothead.
LACEY. Well, Lola Dove was getting everyone all riled up, telling them about the time when you hit her with a brick just t'see if she would bleed.
SUE JACK. Oh, yeah, yeah, well, surprisingly enough that cold, heartless bitch bled a whole lot. Reed's gonna hate me for this when he finds out.
TURNIP. He already knows.
SUE JACK. He does?
TURNIP. He went to try and stop the dancers at the train depot. Guess he didn't make it.
SUE JACK. Well, hell's fire, here he invites me for Christmas and I bring in this whole bag of trouble. What a goddamn mess. God, I'd kill for a drink. Haven't had one in three years.
TURNIP. Well, look. I think I better go try and find Hooker.
SUE JACK. Ooh! Just one straight shot of tequila.
TURNIP. See if he's got anything up his sleeve.
SUE JACK. Or gin, a jolt of gin. (*Turnip exits out the front door, slamming it behind him.*) Okay, okay. I'm fine.
CASSIDY. Well, here's your box for ya. (*Cassidy hands Sue Jack the cardboard box packed with belongings from Sue Jack's past.*)
SUE JACK. Thanks. Thanks a lot. (*Sue Jack stares into the box a moment then takes out a hand mirror.*) Ha! Look here, my silver mirror's cracked. Well, now that's seven years bad luck. Hmm. Wonder when I broke it? God, look at me! How'd all of that sadness ever sink so deep into my face?

Well, let's see what we can do to fix her up. (*Sue Jack takes out some melted rouge and smears it across her cheeks. She becomes disheartened by the effect. She tosses the mirror aside.*) Shouldn't be looking in mirrors. My mama, she shot herself while looking in a full-length mirror. 'Course I'm not like my mama. She went insane due to religious troubles. (*Sue Jack takes out an old bottle of hand lotion, opens it up and smells it.*)

LACEY. Well, I don't know how my mother is; she's not speaking t'me. And I really don't even care 'cause when she was speaking t'me, she never got tired of telling me how I was swivel-hipped and I was never gonna be anything more than some poor man's pudding. Well, I've set out t'prove her wrong. (*To Cassidy.*) So how about your mama? What's she like?

CASSIDY. Well, it's hard t'say 'cause, well she's dead. All of 'em are except me.

SUE JACK. How'd they all die?

CASSIDY. Diptheria. Killed every one of 'em. Then they come out and burned our place down t'ashes. Said it was full of contamination.

LACEY. That's tragic. Having your whole family demolished.

CASSIDY. Of course, my paw, well, I don't know about him, 'cause see I never knowed him. He could be some rich lord living in a castle somewhere or maybe he's just some old bum standing in the breadlines. I'm hoping someday I'll meet him and find out.

SUE JACK. Well, I never met my daddy but if I did, I'd like nothing better than t'spit straight at him.

CASSIDY. Well, all men ain't so bad.

SUE JACK. No. How 'bout your husband? What's he like?

CASSIDY. I, well, I ain't exactly quite got no husband, yet.

SUE JACK. Oh.

CASSIDY. But I will. He's gonna marry me real soon.

SUE JACK. Well, that's good news. (*Pause.*) What sort of wedding you planning?

CASSIDY. Oh, nothing much.

LACEY. Gosh, this sure is a stunning tree, and these berries are just gonna make it look so perky! Don't ya'll think?

SUE JACK. Yeah. You know, you oughta do something

special — dress up at least. Let me look through here. Maybe there's some things you can use. (*Sue Jack rummages through the box.*) God, I'll never forget our wedding. It was St. Patrick's day and it was raining and Thumper Bell . . . Lacey, you remember Thumper Bell? . . .
LACEY. Oh yeh, yeh, the crazy drummer from the Palace.
SUE JACK. Why he kept throwing rice all over us on the wet streets in the rain. Reed and I — we couldn't stop laughing . . . Doesn't that look pretty? (*Sue Jack takes off Cassidy's derby and puts on a fancy hat.*)
LACEY. (*In an attempt to change the focus.*) I've never been married. But I did get left at the church once. Well, actually, it was a home wedding. Oh, we had the house all decorated with colorful flowers and garlands and candlelight. I don't think they'll ever invent anything more romantic than candlelight. Anyway, it's a very funny story — all about how he never came by the house. I guess it makes me out t'look a little foolish. Afterwards, everyone remarked how I took it really well, coming down and joining the party like I did.
CASSIDY. But why didn't he come back t'marry you? What made him not come?
LACEY. I guess he just — Well maybe 'cause I . . . Oh, beats me.
SUE JACK. Here, try on this coat.
CASSIDY. I don't think I better be using your things.
SUE JACK. Look, didn't anybody ever tell you, it's better to give than to receive?
CASSIDY. No.
SUE JACK. Well, occasionally, it's true. (*Throwing the coat around Cassidy.*) There. Lacey, doesn't that look elegant?
LACEY. Well, now that does help!
CASSIDY. Really?
LACEY. My yes. It hides a lot! In fact, I have a dress that'll be just the thing with that coat. I'll run and get it! (*Lacey exits out the side door.*)
SUE JACK. Here's some shoes.
CASSIDY. Why, them's red satin shoes. I always been longing t'have me a pair a them red satin shoes.
SUE JACK. Well, try 'em on.

CASSIDY. No, I, well, I got these different sort of feet. Would it be alright if I tried 'em on upstairs?
SUE JACK. Sure.
CASSIDY. Thanks. (*Cassidy takes the shoes and exits upstairs. Sue Jack goes back to the box. She finds an old deck of cards. She takes out a lace glove and puts it on her hand. She then spots an old teddy bear. She picks it up and holds it with a strange sad wonder. Hooker enters through the front door in a huff. He stops in his tracks when he sees Sue Jack. Sue Jack feels his presence, she drops the toy bear back into the box and turns to face him.*)
SUE JACK. Hi. I, well, I was gonna try and fix up.
HOOKER. No need.
SUE JACK. I'm sorry about running off the dancers.
HOOKER. Yeah.
SUE JACK. I'll try and . . . help out.
HOOKER. I don't think so.
SUE JACK. Well . . . whatever you'd like.
HOOKER. I'd like you outta here.
SUE JACK. I see.
HOOKER. You're like a bad luck charm around my neck. I keep trying t'rip you off and you keep burning my hand.
SUE JACK. I don't wanna burn your hand. I don't mean to.
HOOKER. Then just go.
SUE JACK. I'm not the same as I was Reed. Go on and look at me. You see, I'm not the same. I'm not the same one who kept on hurting you by drinking, and brawling and gambling it all away. And I'm not the young, laughing girl you married with the rosy cheeks and pretty hands. I guess I'm not sure who I am. And, I tell you, it's been making me feel so strange. When I was in prison, the only belonging I had was this old photograph of myself that was taken just before I ran off from home. In it I'm wearing this straw hat decorated with violets and my hair's swept back in a braid and my eyes, they're just . . . shining . . . I used to take out that picture and look at it. I kept on pondering over it. I swear it confused me so much, wondering where she was — that girl in the picture. I could not imagine where she'd departed to — so unknowingly, so unexpectedly. (*A pause.*) Look, I won't drink or yell or fight or shoot pool or bet the roosters or —

HOOKER. Yeah, yeah, and I guess I've heard all that till it's frayed at the edges.
SUE JACK. Please, I don't wanna lose any more. I'm through throwing everything away with both fists.
HOOKER. I'm sorry. I just can't let you in on me ever again.
SUE JACK. Then why did you send for me? Why did you call for me t'come t'you?
HOOKER. . . . I didn't. It was somebody else. It was somebody I'm in kinda a mess with.
SUE JACK. What sort of mess? What somebody?
HOOKER. Look, I really can't afford t'have you flying off the handle.
SUE JACK. I'm alright.
HOOKER. It's just something that happened and I think the best thing is if you just disappeared.
SUE JACK. What are you telling me? Just tell me what you're telling me. (*Cassidy enters at the top of the staircase wearing only one red shoe and holding the other one in her hand.*)
HOOKER. Cassidy, get outta here!
CASSIDY. (*A beat.*) You tell her about us?
HOOKER. Move, do you hear me? Move! Move!
SUE JACK. What are you — what did you — This child?! (*Turnip rushes in the front door. He races behind the counter, grabs a shotgun and heads back towards the front door.*)
TURNIP. Hooker, thank God, come quick! Carmichael's got the whole town riled up. Johnny Montgomery and some of the other guys ya owe money to are taking away everything: the Christmas hog, the Santy Claus mailbox, the Chevy car . . . (*Hooker grabs the shotgun from Turnip and leans it against the wall.*)
HOOKER. Look, we don't need t'start killing people. I can handle Johnny Montgomery. He'll listen to reason. (*Hooker and Turnip exit out the front door.*)
CASSIDY. (*Coming down the staircase.*) You want these things back? (*Sue Jack looks at her, then heads for the counter looking for some liquor.*)
SUE JACK. I want a drink. The real world's getting much too potent. I gotta dilute it with some pure grain alcohol. (*Finding the bottle.*) Ah ha! White mule. I knew I could depend on Mr. Hooker. (*Pouring a drink.*) There now. Let me just

zing one back. (*She throws back a triple shot.*) Ah. So good ol' hooch is legal again. I like that. No more recooking extract, fermenting mash, drinking hair tonic. Wanna jolt?
CASSIDY. No thanks.
SUE JACK. Down the hatch. (*She throws back another big shot.*) So . . . the scum bastard made a play for ya? I mean, you're having his kid, right?
CASSIDY. That's right.
SUE JACK. You know, someone oughta notify the Children's Aid Society or maybe report that s.o.b. to the Morals court. I could do that. I think I'll do that. (*She has another drink.*)
CASSIDY. No, don't do that. He didn't do nothing bad.
SUE JACK. Maybe we'll just have to let the judge decide — like he decided about me. (*She has another drink.*) But personally, I believe that sexual molestation of a young orphan child by a raving drunken idiot is sufficient grounds for criminal prosecution.
CASSIDY. But it weren't like that. Please, ya can't send him off t'no jail!
SUE JACK. Oh, go on and cry all you want. Tears have never been precious to me. Not my own or anybody else's.
CASSIDY. Lady, I'm just asking ya t'do what's right!
SUE JACK. Yeah and just what do you suggest is right?
CASSIDY. Well, it's a clear thing. He don't like you. He don't want you here.
SUE JACK. Did he tell you that?
CASSIDY. Yeah.
SUE JACK. Well, sometimes people don't mean—the things they say.
CASSIDY. I think he means it.
SUE JACK. I wager he doesn't. (*She pours another drink.*)
CASSIDY. Well, I ain't never had a kid by no man before and he tol' me he'd marry me 'cause I ain't raising no stinking bastard.
SUE JACK. If he told you he'd marry 'ya, then he's a no good dirt-crawling liar. See 'cause he's never gonna marry you. He can't. He's married to me.
CASSIDY. Well, he's divorcing you.

SUE JACK. He's what?
CASSIDY. That's right. He's divorcing you and marrying me.
SUE JACK. Oh, he's been dealing you out a very crooked hand.
CASSIDY. Why, you ain't even pretty. They all said how you was so beautiful but you ain't even pretty. I got the bloom of youth and you ain't even pretty.
SUE JACK. Listen to me, you greasy little runt. He's my husband. He loves me. He can't help it. (*Sue Jack picks up the shotgun and aims it in Cassidy's direction.*) And if I were you, I wouldn't go around spreading lies like that. Understand, I'm never gonna get over loving Reed Hooker. 'Cause even when I don't know who in this godless world I am, or was, or ever will be — the one thing I know as sure as the smell of spring rain is that I utterly, hopelessly love that rotten, worthless son of a bitch! (*Throughout the following, Sue Jack fires the shotgun shattering a mirror, light fixtures and the jukebox.*) I want, want, want him like a crazy shrieking, howling dog. I can't live without him! I'll blow out my brains. I'll shoot you to pieces. I'll rip this fucking place t'the ground. But, by God, I gotta have that miserable, lying, double-crossing, one and only love of my broken life! (*Sue Jack stops firing the gun. She looks around a moment then stumbles across the room and gets the whiskey bottle.*) Oh God, look here. I've been misering the bottle. I didn't mean t'do that. (*Lacey runs in with the dress.*)
LACEY. What in the world . . . ? Are y'all alright? Oh, my Lord, look here. (*Lacey trips and falls as Turnip and Hooker come in together. They have been in a fight. Turnip is carrying Hooker; he is a bloody mess.*)
TURNIP. Thank God, Sue Jack. Thank God for those shots. You scared those bastards away. They almost murdered Hooker. (*Turnip sits Hooker down.*)
HOOKER. Yeah, thanks. Thanks a lot. (*Hooker looks up. He sees the damage, He sees the liquor bottle in Sue Jack's hand.*) What's all this? You've shot this place to shit. My jukebox. Look at my jukebox. (*Hooker rises, fury begins to blind him.*) Why you stupid slut — (*What follows is an all-out, lowdown and*

rutty brawl. The other characters are all somehow thrust in and out and back in and out of this massive free-for-all battle that leaves the place in total shambles.)

SUE JACK. Don't you ever hit me.

HOOKER. Hit you? Hit you?! I'm gonna kill you! I'm gonna rip your head off your shoulders.

SUE JACK. Stay away. You stay away!

HOOKER. I'm sick of you ruining my life! You're not gonna ruin it any more!

SUE JACK. I'm ruining your life? That's rich. That's damn rich. You're the worthless, two-timing bastard who messed out on me.

HOOKER. And what the hell else was I gonna do when you shut me out with you drinking for weeks on end, staying binged out of your goddamned mind, gambling away every nickel we ever had?!

SUE JACK. Yeah, well, at least I never messed out on you.

HOOKER. That's a damned lie!

SUE JACK. Don't call me a liar!

HOOKER. (*Running on.*) Why, you stayed for five weeks out in that trash can shack getting drunk and screwing your cousin, the undertaker.

SUE JACK. That was different! That was family!

HOOKER. Bullshit!

SUE JACK. You know good and well I never loved him. But I saw all those poems you wrote to Caroline Carmichael.

HOOKER. You read my poems?!

SUE JACK. That one about how she smelled!

HOOKER. I never said you could read my poems! I'm gonna butcher you for that!

SUE JACK. Go ahead! Poke out my red eyes. Tear out my dying hair. I'm a sickening, wretched, worthless glob of pulp. But at least I never crawled so low as t'mercilessly abduct and rape a poor runt of an orphan child!

HOOKER. Let me at her! I'm gonna shred open your face! I'm gonna tear out your decaying heart! (*Hooker catches Sue Jack. They struggle passionately.*) You bitch!

SUE JACK. You bastard!

HOOKER. I'm glad they stuck you in that jail. I pray you go back! I pray you get nothing but bread and water and blood

caked rot for the rest of your useless life! (*Hooker slings Sue Jack to the floor. Sue Jack gets to her feet and grabs the rifle. She comes toward him swinging it at him.*)
SUE JACK. I'm glad I threw Caroline Carmichael over that balcony rail. I'm glad she broke both her arms and gashed up her face. Let that serve as fair warning to any other whore I find in your bed! Fair warning to all whores! (*Hooker grabs the rifle away from her. They start to strangle each other.*)
HOOKER. I'm gonna kill you.
SUE JACK. I'm gonna kill you.
HOOKER. I hate your guts.
SUE JACK. I hate your guts.
HOOKER. You bitch.
SUE JACK. You bastard.
HOOKER. You bitch.
SUE JACK. You bastard. You—
HOOKER. You . . .
SUE JACK. You . . . (*They both collapse on the floor. It is a double knockout. Music B comes up as the lights fade to black.*)*

END OF ACT I

---

*See Special Note on copyright page.

ACT II

Scene 1

The stage is dark. Music A: "I Need A Little Sugar In My Bowl"*—a low down rinky dink blues tune plays on a record player. It is about eight o'clock in the evening on the same day.

HOOKER's VOICE. Okay, try the switch. (*A little toy village is lit up on the dark stage.*) It's working!
TURNIP. Yeah.
HOOKER. The whole village. (*A beat.*) All lit up. All aglow. Turnip?
TURNIP. Huh?
HOOKER. She gone yet?
TURNIP. Not yet.
HOOKER. Get her outta here. I don't wanna lay eyes on her ever again. (*A beat.*) You hear me?
TURNIP. Yeah. Can I get the lights now?
HOOKER. Go ahead. (*We see that Hooker has a bump on his head, a black eye, and his hand is wrapped in gauze. He is dressed in tails. Turnip wears a baggy suit and a skinny tie. The damage from this morning's brawl has basically been repaired or hidden under the decorations that have been put up for this evening's extravaganza. The record player and three or four large stacks of records sit on the counter top along with a huge punch bowl and coffee pot and a plate of cookies. A few empty chairs are lined up against the wall. Throughout the following Hooker and Turnip line the rest of the stacked up chairs up against the wall.*)
TURNIP. Hooker.
HOOKER. Huh?
TURNIP. I don't think this is gonna work.
HOOKER. Well, then we'll toss it. There're plenty more swell ones. We've got stacks of 'em. (*Hooker removes the record and tosses it into a cardboard box.*)

---

*See Special Note on copyright page.

TURNIP. I don't just mean these old records. I mean the whole thing. The whole opening of the Lucky Spot.
HOOKER. What about it?
TURNIP. I really think we oughta put off the Grand Opening. I mean we don't have no music or no taxi dancers; our electric sign's all broke. Face it — the cards are stacking up against us.
HOOKER. Look, we can't put off the grand opening. I owe too damn much money. There're people out there who are waiting to break both my legs. I need anything we can make tonight t'help fend off the wolves.
TURNIP. We're gonna be opening ourselves up to all sorts of ridicule.
HOOKER. Be that as it may.
TURNIP. I mean Cassidy can't be out here dancing around for ten cents a ticket. (*Indicating a huge stomach.*) She's out t'here, for Christ sake.
HOOKER. Are you telling me how to run my affairs?!
TURNIP. No, it's just . . . well, ya oughtta think about her feelings sometimes. She does have 'em.
HOOKER. Hey, I'm not a blind man. I know how I've treated her. I know I'm a bilge bag. I hate my own goddamn guts.
TURNIP. I don't mean t'criticize you—
HOOKER. Go ahead! It's clear I'm culpable for the preposterous condition she's in. I should have taken that chestnut mare, but I took Cassidy instead. (*A beat.*) She had such a sad face; a woebegone countenance. I hoped I could change that face. Instead I've made it worse.
TURNIP. The main thing is she doesn't want the kid to be born out a bastard.
HOOKER. Right. Right. So I'm supposed t'marry her.
TURNIP. Yeah. Well, listen, I don't know much about these things; so correct me if I'm mistaken, but from the looks of it you and Sue Jack are kinda on the outs — But even so if you needed someone to, well, — about Cassidy, I mean — I could take— (*Cassidy comes walking down the stairs. She is dressed in the clothes Sue Jack and Lacey helped her put together in Act I. Her hair is fixed in curls under a hat.*) Oh. Hi, Cassidy.
CASSIDY. Hi.

HOOKER. Hi.
CASSIDY. (*A beat.*) I look okay?
TURNIP. Yeah. Nice.
HOOKER. Your hair's kinda sticking out some around the sides. Come here and let me fix it. (*Cassidy goes to Hooker. He starts working with her hair.*) Hold still. (*A beat.*) Does that pull?
CASSIDY. No.
HOOKER. (*Still working on her hair.*) So . . . Uh, you had any ideas about how t'do this wedding?
CASSIDY. (*A beat.*) No; just signing the papers.
HOOKER. You interested in a cake or a white dress or throwing rice or anything?
CASSIDY. I . . . no.
HOOKER. Maybe we could go out t'eat at a restaurant or something afterwards . . . if you wanted to.
CASSIDY. (*Nodding yes.*) Uh huh.
HOOKER. We'll do that then. There. That looks better — don't lose those hairpins. Gotta go out and . . . work on the sign. (*Hooker exits out the front door. Cassidy turns to Turnip. Both of them are white.*)
CASSIDY. You hear that? He's talking about my marriage t'him. He remembered all about it. He's gonna marry me. He's gonna do it.
TURNIP. I reckon so.
CASSIDY. He's gonna keep his promise. Just like you said. Why you're the one that promised me he'd keep his promise. You're the one! Oh, thank you, Turnip! (*Cassidy grabs Turnip and kisses him.*)
TURNIP. Well, don't kiss me about it! He's only marrying ya on the rebound.
CASSIDY. The what?
TURNIP. The rebound, the rebound, from Sue Jack. Ya don't just want him t'marry ya on the rebound, do ya?
CASSIDY. Yeah. I sure do. I sure do.
TURNIP. Yeah, I reckon so. (*Lacey sticks her head in from the kitchen door.*) Oh, Lacey, come on in! Come on in!
LACEY. (*Over her shoulder.*) The coast is clear. (*Lacey enters the room, Sue Jack follows behind her.*)
TURNIP. (*Not noticing Sue Jack.*) We're just having the big-

gest celebration! Hooker's proposed marriage t'Cassidy. He's made a definite public proposal! Ain't life a boon! (*Turnip and Cassidy see Sue Jack.*) Oh I — (*Cassidy gasps at the sight of her and runs to hide under a table. Sue Jack wears makeup and has restyled her hair. She is dressed in a glamourous tight fitted dress from her past. She has a bruise on her cheek. Lacey is dressed in an old evening gown with dirty hand prints around the waist.*)

SUE JACK. It's alright. It's fine. (*To Cassidy.*) Hey, come on out from under there. I'm not gonna hurt ya. Honestly. Come on out now. (*Cassidy slowly crawls out from under the table.*) Look, I'm sorry I shot at ya this morning. Okay? I guess I just — stepped outta line a little bit.

TURNIP. So, any luck with the phone calling?

SUE JACK. Oh, sure. I've got several friends who want me t'spend Christmas with them. I've just got to decide if I'm looking for a real sophisticated kind of Christmas or a big warm family sort of time, or maybe I just want t'spend a quiet, peaceful Christmas with a few intimate friends.

TURNIP. Yeah. Well, it sounds pretty nice.

SUE JACK. I tell ya, I feel refreshed. All that stupid, miserable hope I've let eat at me for so long has finally been beaten t'death. Reed and I are disbanded. We were never quite right for each other. This morning we tried to . . . kill each other. (*A beat.*) I'm renewed. I'm free t'be a globe-trotter once again. T'live by my wits. Ah, how I love a changing panorama.

TURNIP. Yeah — well — you look real beautiful.

SUE JACK. Right. Gotta impress my old acquaintances. Oh, by the way, Turnip, do you have any idea whatever happened to Thumper Bell? I thought I might try and give him a call — make sure someone remembered to invite him up for Christmas.

TURNIP. No, I — Well, Thumper, he died. I'm sorry t'tell ya. Happened last spring. He, ah, stopped in an alleyway t'pick up some change and got hit by a falling flower box.

SUE JACK. Oh. Rotten luck. Poor Thumper. Well, I'll get my things and be heading out.

TURNIP. Yeah. (*Sue Jack exits out the side door to the bungalows.*) She really get any of those folks she was calling?

LACEY. Didn't sound like it to me.
TURNIP. She's been on the phone all afternoon. Seems like somebody would've come through for her.
LACEY. It's so sad. She'll be spending Christmas all alone.
TURNIP. Sometimes life makes me wanna puke. One stroke of really bad luck and people just can't never seem t'recover.
LACEY. You mean about their little boy.
TURNIP. Yeah, after he died things went hateful crazy.
CASSIDY. Sue Jack and Hooker had some child together?
TURNIP. Yeah. His name was Andrew. (*A beat.*) They called him Andy.
CASSIDY. How old was he?
TURNIP. (*Indicating the height of a 2–3 year old child.*) 'Bout this old. You know small.
CASSIDY. And he died?
TURNIP. Yeah. Ran out in the road and got hit by some automobile. They say he was chasing after a hummingbird.
LACEY. Oooh! I'd just run and jump straight off a cliff if I didn't have a place t'go to on Christmas Day.
TURNIP. Hell, I might just do it anyway.
CASSIDY. (*A beat.*) Well, why don't she just stay on here for Christmas?
TURNIP. Here?
LACEY. You'd want her here?
CASSIDY. I wouldn't mind.
LACEY. Well, if you don't mind—
TURNIP. Hooker refuses t'ever lay eyes on her again.
CASSIDY. Maybe if we just explain—
LACEY. I mean after all, we certainly could use an extra taxi dancer.
TURNIP. Hooker ain't listening t'reason. He's trying t'open up this dance hall with two dancers and no music. Claims he needs the money. Why, we'd make more money selling apples on a street corner. But he can't see it. Ah, I don't care! What does any of it matter?! All these miserable people butting around. Trying so hard. For what?! Before it's all over everyone of 'em's gonna be stone cold dead! Absolutely everyone of 'em. (*Snapping his fingers.*) Dead! Dead! Dead! So what the hell are they all sweating?! That's what I'd

relish t'know! Oooh!! What a low down rutty rotten little game we're all playing. It ain't like checkers. In checkers somebody wins and somebody loses. It's clear-cut. But playing this other — we're all big-time losers; everyone of us. No ringing in the cold deck, no aces up the sleeves, no hold outs. Just stacking up piles and piles of chips, t'give 'em all away. All losers! Everyone of us — Christ, what a racket.
LACEY. (*A beat.*) Now there's conversation for ya. There's genuine, sparkling, earnest conversation.
CASSIDY. Well, it kinda makes me wanna go beat out all my brains.
LACEY. That's what real conversation'll do t'ya.
CASSIDY. Well, I don't like the feeling. Thinking about how this thing's gonna be dead here it ain't even been born yet. Why it all just gives me goose chills straight up my thighs.
LACEY. I, on the other hand, appreciate a man who will converse with a lady. Tell me, Turnip, do you have any further conversation that I may partake in?
TURNIP. I, well, I do have things to say. Just generally I don't say 'em.
CASSIDY. Look, I'm going out front t'talk t'Hooker. I wanna explain t'him about that lady staying on here through Christmas day. (*A beat.*) I'm going on out t'ask him. (*Cassidy looks uneasily at Turnip and Lacey who are staring at each other.*)
TURNIP. Well . . . 'Bye.
LACEY. Bye.
CASSIDY. Yeah. 'Bye. (*Cassidy exits out the front door. Lacey continues to look at Turnip with wet, listening eyes.*)
TURNIP. . . . I'm not stupid. A lot of people think of me as stupid. My brothers they always called me stupid. But I wasn't. I thought a lot. Mostly about things they never even featured. Like don't always go around making fun of people with harelips 'cause it don't do no good and they can't help it no how.
LACEY. (*A pause.*) You know what you've got? Sensitivity. Real sensitivity.
TURNIP. You're probably right. What can I do about it?
LACEY. You're — You're asking me a vital question in a prolonged conversation. Oh my, oh my, oh my. (*Lacey stumbles around and manages to fall to the floor.*) See here! Didn't I

tell ya? It's the bird bones in my ankles. (*Turnip helps Lacey to her feet as Sue Jack comes in carrying the dilapidated cardboard box with her belongings. She wears black lace gloves and a black hat with berries.*)
SUE JACK. Hi.
LACEY. Oh hi.
TURNIP. Hi. (*A beat.*) Can you handle that?
SUE JACK. Sure. Look—I—Well, here's some Christmas things. (*Sue Jack sets down the box. She takes out some gifts wrapped in dirty tissue paper from the large handbag.*) They're nothing, really. Just some things I made while I was in—there. I don't know; I thought somebody might want 'em. Turnip. (*Sue Jack hands a package to Turnip.*)
TURNIP. Thanks.
SUE JACK. Here, Lacey.
LACEY. Thanks, Sugar. I love Christmas presents.
TURNIP. Look, that box is falling apart. Let me go out back here and find you a flour sack or something t'make it easier for ya t'carry. (*Turnip picks up the box.*)
SUE JACK. Don't trouble yourself.
TURNIP. Ain't no trouble. Come on. (*Turnip and Sue Jack exit into the kitchen. Lacey quickly unwraps her gift. It is an embroidered Christmas bell.*)
LACEY. A bell. (*A beat.*) Jingle, jingle, jingle. (*Hooker and Cassidy enter from the front door. Hooker carries a toolbox.*)
HOOKER. Look, I'm about on my last leg around here and I refuse t'have her hanging around just t'kick it out from under me.
CASSIDY. But she ain't gonna kick ya. I swear she ain't.
LACEY. It's Christmas Eve. Give her one more chance.
HOOKER. No. (*Sue Jack and Turnip enter from the kitchen. Sue Jack's belongings have been transferred into a burlap flour sack.*) And what's all this crap? Who brought over these dirty Christmas presents?
SUE JACK. I did. (*Hooker turns to see Sue Jack.*)
HOOKER. Oh. (*A beat.*) Well, we don't need 'em. We've got plenty of our own.
SUE JACK. Alright. (*Sue Jack takes the Christmas presents and slowly puts them in the burlap sack. To Hooker.*) Look, I'll write where I'm staying. You can send the divorce papers on and

I'll sign 'em. (*A beat.*) Well, goodbye everybody. Have a good Christmas.
TURNIP. Goodbye, Sue Jack. Merry Christmas.
LACEY. I — I love my bell. You have a real good Christmas now.
SUE JACK. Yeah, you, too. Goodbye now.
CASSIDY. Goodbye. (*Sue Jack exits out the front door. Cassidy, Lacey and Turnip stare sadly after her, then turn and look at Hooker in stony silence.*)
HOOKER. So enough goldbricking. Everyone back t'work. Tonight's our big night! (*Looking at his watch.*) Come on everybody, as of now we're open for business! (*Turnip is opening the present Sue Jack gave him. Lacey and Cassidy gather around him.*)
LACEY. So what'd she give ya?
TURNIP. Mittens with snowmen on 'em.
CASSIDY. Oh look, ain't it sad, one of 'em's melting. (*Hooker comes over to them; he grabs the mittens from Turnip.*)
HOOKER. Let me see those! (*Hooker roughly puts one of the mittens on his hand, then pulls it off. He takes the mittens and throws them out the front door. He yells to Sue Jack, who is headed down the road.*) Hey you got a lot of nerve walking outta here like this! You know damn good and well we only have two dancers for tonight! And it's all 'cause of you showing your face! But don't let it bother ya! Just run off t'your fancy Christmas parties. Forget about us! We'll do just fine all on our own! (*Hooker turns and comes back inside the room, slamming the front door shut. After a moment Sue Jack enters through the front door.*)
SUE JACK. Alright, Hooker. I'll do the Lucky Spot this one favor. After all, it is Christmas.
HOOKER. Fine! But once we get squared — I don't even wanna remember your face. (*Music B — the trumpet solo from "I Must Have That Man"* — comes up. Sue Jack slowly starts to remove her hat and gloves as the lights fade to blackout.*)

END OF SCENE 1

---

*See Special Note on copyright page.

ACT II

Scene 2

The lights fade up. Music B fades into Music C: "Twelfth Street Rag."* It plays on the phonograph. Sue Jack sits in the window seat doing string tricks. Lacey and Cassidy dance awkwardly together. It is two to three hours later on the same evening.

LACEY. (*Instructing Cassidy.*) Don't look down. Up! Up! Smile! Look happy! Come on, be peppy! Get some zing! Bubble! Twirl out! (*Lacey twirls Cassidy out across the room. Cassidy crashes into the bar. Lacey removes the needle from the record.*)
CASSIDY. It ain't much use. I don't know how t'move around t'this music.
LACEY. Don't worry you'll get the hang of it. See 'cause, your main problem's not the dancing — it's simply that you're not used t'being in the limelight.
CASSIDY. Nah, I ain't used t'being in no limelight.
LACEY. Well, being in the limelight's easy. All ya gotta do is learn how t'emphasize your striking features. That way ya won't fade out.
CASSIDY. I don't wanna fade out.
LACEY. Well then, we'll emphasize your eyes. You've got very pretty eyes. Come here, we'll just darken 'em up some. (*Lacey gets an eyeliner pencil from her evening bag and starts darkening Cassidy's eyes.*) Take me. For awhile I wasn't getting the dances; so I moved over and started in corner dancing. A place where I could really shine.
CASSIDY. What's corner dancing?
LACEY. Well, just dancing in a dark corner. You know, where you start allowing neck kissing, ear biting and body pressing.
CASSIDY. Gosh, are they gonna be biting on my ears?
LACEY. Oh no, you've got years before ya have t'get into corner dancing. You've got the bloom of youth.
CASSIDY. That's good. (*From outside the front door we hear*

---
*See Special Note on copyright page.

Hooker's voice calling through a megaphone in the distance.)
HOOKER. (*Offstage.*) Grand opening! Lucky Spot Dance Hall! Come one! Come all!
SUE JACK. Oh God. Look at Reed out there calling to cars through that megaphone. He's making a laughing stock.
HOOKER. Free prizes! Come one! Come all!
LACEY. Well, we do need the business.
HOOKER. (*Offstage.*) Merry Christmas! Ho, ho, ho!
CASSIDY. I sure hope some people come.
SUE JACK. Would you come to a place with a madman standing out front yelling at ya through a megaphone? (*Turnip enters through the front door.*)
TURNIP. Hey, Lacey, Hooker wants ya t'come out front and do your cartwheels.
SUE JACK. Oh good Christ.
TURNIP. He says maybe you can arrest the attention of some of them passing cars.
LACEY. Well, okay. But I better stretch out a little. (*Stretching.*) One and two and— (*She falls to the floor.*) Oops! My wayward ankles again.
TURNIP. Here, let me help ya up.
LACEY. (*To Turnip.*) Why thank you, Turnip. You're such a lamb. I just can't keep my eyes off your eyes. (*Turnip escorts Lacey out the front door. Cassidy looks after them perturbed. Sue Jack goes back to playing with the string. Cassidy hikes her skirt up over her knees.*)
CASSIDY. Look here, my knees got dirt all on 'em. I have real trouble keeping clean. (*She spits on her hand and starts scrubbing her knees.*) Mr. Pete, he used t'call me a godless bag a stench. Mr. Pete's the man I was with before. He's the one Hooker won me offa. And that was a lucky day for me. See 'cause when I was with Mr. Pete practically all he'd ever give me t'eat was cow feed. Why, if fact be known, the man was downright feeble-minded. Look here where he branded me with his holy cross. (*Cassidy hikes up her skirt and reveals a cross branded to her inner thigh.*)
SUE JACK. My God.
CASSIDY. He's always telling me how all fired holy he is. Him being a member of the Church of Innocent Blood— and me being a godless bag a stench. Lord, my life ain't never

been no good till now. But here, well, we have supper together every night. It's the most I ever felt like a family.
SUE JACK. Yeah. Some people need that I guess.
CASSIDY. Uh huh. Look, I just wanted t'tell ya — it wasn't like what you was saying this morning. See Hooker, he wasn't all mean and drunk or nothing like that the night when it happened.
SUE JACK. Jesus, I don't care how it happened. It doesn't matter how it happened. (*A beat.*) Okay, so are you gonna tell me how it happened?
CASSIDY. Well, used to be I'd hear him at night yelling out and gasping for air and such. I reckoned him t'be having bad dreams; so I started rushing down t'his room t'wake him up. I'd bring him water t'drink and wet down his forehead with a cool rag. Afterward he'd never go back t'sleep, but he'd send me back on t'bed telling me how I needed t'get my rest. Then one time he just up and says for me t'stop coming in with the water. Says for me just t'stay put and let him be. And I done that for some nights. I sure didn't like listening t'him, but I stood it. Then this one night I hear such crying, like it's coming from some sick, dying animal. Well, I can't find no control for myself, but t'run in with the water. I wake him up and I wash off his face and I hold him so hard and I say, "Don't be scared no more. I can make ya feel better. I know some ways t'make ya feel better." And I did too, from being out on the trail so long with Mr. Pete. Next day though he moves all my things up t'the attic. (*A beat.*) He locks me up there at nights now. Turnip, he'll come by and unlatch the door in the mornings. I'm hoping all that's gonna be changed once we're married. But I don't really know. Only thing I do know is this thing ain't being born out no bastard. See 'cause bastards they don't deserve nothing. Hooker'll be good to it. Once this skinny kid, he fell outta that mossy tree out front and split up his lip real good. Hooker done this trick with a nickel t'make him shut up crying then he let him keep the nickel.
SUE JACK. He did? He did that nickel trick?

---

*See Special Note on copyright page.

CASSIDY. I ain't never seen anything like it.
SUE JACK. (*A pause.*) Yeah, well . . . sometimes I wonder . . . I really do wonder. (*A pause.*) The whole world's in trouble. So what's the use? Huh? (*Sue Jack gets up and starts pacing around the room with crazed exuberance.*) I mean, maybe ya gotta just toss in your hand, pay off your debts; stand up and leave the goddamn table.
CASSIDY. Leave the table?
SUE JACK. Yeah. It's worth a go. Gotta go. Letting go! (*Sue Jack puts Music B* on the record player. She starts dancing with a wild crazed passion.*)
CASSIDY. Gosh! Why're ya dancing around?
SUE JACK. (*Still dancing.*) I don't know. I just feel crazy and lighthearted. Like when you're standing on the very edge of a mountain cliff and you're kicking your legs up t'the sky. (*Sue Jack stands on the bar and starts kicking up her legs.*)
CASSIDY. I feel lighthearted too. (*The women dance around the room.*) It's kinda like we're friends or something. (*Turnip enters carrying Lacey who is whining and laughing.*)
LACEY. Ooh. Ooh. Ow
TURNIP. (*To Lacey.*) There, there, now.
LACEY. (*Gaily.*) I fell down again. I'm always falling—(*They stop and watch the women dance.*)
TURNIP. Why are y'all so happy?
CASSIDY. We're dancing on the edge of a cliff. (*Hooker enters. He wears a silk hat and carries a megaphone. He stops the music.*)
HOOKER. An extravaganza! This was supposed to be an extravaganza! Instead it's a farce, it's a flop. A dream so shattered I can't even remember what the pieces were.
CASSIDY. Oh, don't get discouraged. We still got a roof over our heads and tomorrow we're having ham for Christmas dinner. Things ain't so bad.
HOOKER. Right. Right. Sometimes I just have t'stop myself and take time out t'be grateful I'm not a one-eyed paraplegic with severe brain damage dancing in a cardboard hat. (*A beat.*) Damn. I didn't wanna have the Lucky Spot turning out t'be just like any other roadside attraction.
SUE JACK. I don't think you're in any danger of that!

HOOKER. That's right! Make fun! Laugh at me! You've always got all the smart answers.
SUE JACK. I was just joking.
HOOKER. I'm not a joke.
SUE JACK. Come on, Reed, the whole world's a joke. Consider yourself a real sucker when being taken seriously becomes any sort of goal at all.
HOOKER. Well now if this world is such a goddamn hilarious funny little joke, then please, you tell me, why the hell don't I feel like laughing?
CASSIDY. (*Looking out the window.*) Look, somebody's coming!
HOOKER. Hot damn! We're in business!
LACEY. Oh my God. He's coming up the walk.
HOOKER. Quick, get on some music. (*Turnip puts on Music C — "Twelfth Street Rag."**)
CASSIDY. Where's my hat? I need my hat!
LACEY. Look on your head, silly.
HOOKER. Everybody line up over here. Look pretty!
LACEY. Get peppy, girls! Get peppy!
TURNIP. Okay, here're the ties. I've got the ties.
HOOKER. No, you sell the tickets; I'll sell the ties.
TURNIP. Okay.
HOOKER. No, no I'll sell the tickets, you sell the ties.
TURNIP. Okay, right.
CASSIDY. Here he comes! (*Carmichael enters through the front door. He is dressed in evening attire. At the sight of Carmichael everyone's energy drops except for Lacey who is too busy doing her cartwheels.*)
SUE JACK. HOOKER, TURNIP. Shit.
LACEY. Dance? Dance? Wanna dance?
CARMICHAEL. Yes, I'll have a ticket. Just one, thanks. I'll pass on the neckties for now. (*Carmichael buys his ticket from Hooker, then walks over to the line of women. He scrutinizes them as he paces back and forth. He finally hands his ticket to Sue Jack. They start to dance.*) So the place seems to be hopping. It's a

---

*See Special Note on copyright page.

shame about the jukebox. But you know these old race records of Davenport's aren't so bad. (*The record sticks.*) Kinda scratchy. But not so bad. (*A beat as the record continues to repeat itself.*) Not so bad. Not so bad. Not so bad. (*Turnip finally picks the needle up off the record. Sue Jack and Carmichael continue to dance in silence.*) It's always such a pleasure dancing with you. It's like dancing with a dream. (*Hooker rings the bell.*)
HOOKER. Okay, the dance is over. I said it's over. Look, you came by here to gloat; so you've gloated. Now get out.
CARMICHAEL. Listen to me a minute. You're a smart man. Try to keep a clear head. You know this place will never make it. Do yourself a favor, let me take it off your hands.
HOOKER. I don't get you, Carmichael. Just why are you so dead set t'get at this place?
CARMICHAEL. The truth is I promised my father I'd get it for him. As sort of a Christmas gift. (*Indicating Sue Jack.*) He couldn't stand the idea of her being here after that mess with Caroline. I don't blame him much. Here're the papers. If you sign 'em it'll let everyone off the hook.
HOOKER. I don't know. I'm not real keen on the idea.
CARMICHAEL. Believe me, it's a fair price.
SUE JACK. Well, now that worries me. (*Hooker takes the papers down to a table. He motions to Turnip to come with him.*)
HOOKER. (*To Turnip.*) What d'you think?
TURNIP. Gosh, it's hard t'say. After all the badmouthing he's been doing about us around town I really don't know that we have a frank chance a making it here.
CARMICHAEL. You don't have a blind chance.
HOOKER. I don't know. I got a strong feeling this place isn't realizing its full potential. I mean, look at that painted horse over there. Why it's — otherworldly.
CARMICHAEL. I think you're living in a rosy dream world.
SUE JACK. I smell fish.
CARMICHAEL. What?
SUE JACK. I said I smell fish.
CASSIDY. There's somebody out there. Somebody else is coming.
LACEY. A patron! It's a patron. A real live patron.

HOOKER. Turnip, music! (*Music D—"King Joe"*—starts to play.*)
CARMICHAEL. Look, this is a fair offer, but you'll have to accept it, right now.
HOOKER. I—No.
LACEY. How're my lips?
SUE JACK. Red, real red!
CARMICHAEL. Be reasonable. One patron's not going to change anything.
HOOKER. Excuse me now, I'm working.
LACEY. Get perky, everybody! Get perky!
CARMICHAEL. This price goes down three hundred dollars an hour.
HOOKER. No deal, Carmichael. No deal!
SUE JACK. That's a damn good tune.
HOOKER. It's a very pretty tune.
CARMICHAEL. Make that five hundred dollars an hour or fraction thereof.
HOOKER. I said, no deal.
SUE JACK. I do like that pretty tune.
LACEY. Dance. Dance. Wanna dance. (*Lacey turns cartwheels. The patron, Sam, enters. He is a thin shy man in his 60's dressed in clean simple clothes. His face and hands are weatherbeaten from years of farming.*)
HOOKER. Welcome, welcome, welcome.
SAM. 'Evening.
HOOKER. Come right in, sir. Come right on in. Now would ya like t'rent a necktie? I'm afraid they are required.
SAM. Alright.
HOOKER. That'll be fifteen cents.
TURNIP. (*Echoing.*) Fifteen cents.
HOOKER. No, that's twenty cents . . .
TURNIP. (*Echoing.*) Twenty cents . . .
SAM. (*After a beat.*) Alright.
HOOKER. How 'bout this red one. It's very festive. It's just your particular style. Turnip, help the gentleman out with his tie. (*Turnip puts the tie on Sam.*) Now how many dance tickets would you like?

---

*See Special Note on copyright page.

SAM. How many ya reckon I'll need?
HOOKER. I don't know. Fifty? A hundred maybe?
SAM. How 'bout a dollar's worth. That's about all I got.
HOOKER. Alright. Fine. Here're your tickets. Now you go on and select any one of our beautiful dance teachers t'be your partner.
SAM. I pick?
HOOKER. Yes, you pick.
SAM. Which one do I pick?
HOOKER. Anyone you want. All of our girls make a wonderful partner. They all have very special qualities.
SAM. (*A beat.*) It's sure hard t'pick.
HOOKER. Well, just go on and point t'one of 'em. It's all the same. Go ahead. Point. (*Sam hesitates a moment then points to Cassidy.*)
CASSIDY. He's pointing at me. Hey, mister, you're pointing at me.
SAM. What do I do now?
HOOKER. Give her your ticket and dance. Dance, quick, before the bell rings. (*Sam hands Cassidy his ticket. Cassidy and Sam make an awkward attempt at dancing.*)
SAM. I hope my hands ain't too clammy for ya.
CASSIDY. No, it's okay. (*A beat.*) I—
SAM. What?
CASSIDY. Nothing. I'm just glad I was picked. I ain't never been picked. (*Music D swells up then comes back down. Music E—"Sweet Lorraine"—comes up.* The lights change indicating the passing of time. Sue Jack and Lacey are now dancing together. Hooker watches Sue Jack from the stairs. Cassidy and Sam continue dancing. Turnip stands by the record player. Carmichael goes outside and lights up a cigarette. To Sam.*) Musta been hard on your wife, having t'be blind all her life. Me, I don't even like the dark. I'm afraid of it.
SAM. Well, she used t'tell me, of everything in the world, the two things she most wanted t'see was the face of a person and a tree. But she said she was happy just being here on this earth.
CASSIDY. How long ago was it she died?

---
*See Special Note on copyright page.

SAM. Been almost five weeks now.
CASSIDY. You miss her?
SAM. Oh yeah. She loved watermelon. I used t'slice it up for her and pick out all the seed. (*Lacey twirls over to Turnip. Hooker stares at Sue Jack from across the room. She stares back.*)
LACEY. Hi Turnip.
TURNIP. Hi. You, ah, you wanna dance?
LACEY. Sure. You got a ticket?
TURNIP. I — no.
LACEY. Well, I gotta have a ticket.
TURNIP. Oh. Well, I guess I don't have the monty t'buy one.
LACEY. (*A beat.*) Sorry, then. It's the rules.
SAM. (*To Cassidy.*) Is that your fellow?
CASSIDY. Who?
SAM. The young guy putting on the records. The one you've got your eye on.
CASSIDY. (*Indicating Turnip.*) Him? Oh no. He's just some nitwit. (*Indicating Hooker.*) I'm engaged t'the man on the staircase. (*A beat.*) He's in love with me. (*Sue Jack steps into the outdoor area. Carmichael is sitting on a bench smoking.*)
CARMICHAEL. You wanna drink?
SUE JACK. I quit.
CARMICHAEL. You can't stand me, can you?
SUE JACK. Not really.
CARMICHAEL. It's funny but I like you.
SUE JACK. Well, you can afford to.
CARMICHAEL. There're two things I've always wanted to do to you. One of them was beat you in a game of cards.
SUE JACK. You're a slime, Whitt. A real slime.
CARMICHAEL. Come on. Play cards with me. Let's gamble. Come on. I wanna beat you.
SUE JACK. Shit. (*Sue Jack turns to go inside.*)
CARMICHAEL. Don't go inside.
SUE JACK. Screw you. Go buy some tickets if you wanna take up my time. My time is money. Big money. (*Sue Jack goes inside. Carmichael follows her. Hooker watches them both. Turnip is ringing the bell, indicating that Dance E is over. Lacey rushes up to Sam and Cassidy and throws herself between them.*)

LACEY. (*To Sam.*) Oh, dance with me. Next time let me be your partner. Let me be your one.

SAM. I'm getting kinda tuckered. Maybe I'll sit this one out.

LACEY. Fine, sit with me. I'm a sympathetic listener. (*She pulls him over to a table and starts plucking off tickets from his roll.*) I know how t'show ya a good time. (*Carmichael comes up to Hooker who has been staring at Sue Jack.*)

CARMICHAEL. I'd like some more tickets. (*Carmichael takes out a large bill.*)

HOOKER. What're you still doing here?

CARMICHAEL. Waiting for you t'crack.

HOOKER. Forget about it. I'm not gonna crack. This place could be something great. Look at that lonely guy over there. He's having a damn ball. See that? (*Hooker, Carmichael and Turnip all turn and watch Lacey chewing on Sam's red tie.*)

CARMICHAEL. Ah yes, yes. How very picturesque. (*Music F—"Honeysuckle Rose"*—starts to play. Carmichael turns and heads over to Sue Jack. Carmichael offers her a reel of tickets. She takes them. Hooker can't take his eyes off of them. Turnip continues to watch Lacey and Sam. Cassidy looks from Hooker to Turnip and back again.*)

SUE JACK. (*Dancing and laughing.*) Oh that music sends me someplace, someplace — I wish I could tell you where. Take me away! Please, take me away!

HOOKER. Oh sweet Jesus. Holy Jesus.

TURNIP. What?

HOOKER. Look at Sue dancing. I'll never get over her. There's nobody else like her. Nobody else.

TURNIP. What're you saying?

HOOKER. I love her. I want her. Can't help it. Never could.

TURNIP. I don't get you. (*Cassidy walks over to Hooker and Turnip.*)

CASSIDY. (*To Hooker.*) Hi. You wanna dance?

HOOKER. No. I'm going outside. (*Hooker exits out the side door.*)

TURNIP. (*To Cassidy.*) I'll dance with ya.

---

*See Special Note on copyright page.

CASSIDY. Why don't ya go ask Lacey t'dance? She's the one you're so fond of. (*Cassidy turns and walks away.*)
LACEY. (*To Sam.*) You like my hair?
SAM. It's the color of spun gold.
LACEY. It's all natural. You can feel it if ya want to. Go ahead. Run your fingers right through it.
SAM. (*To Lacey as he fondles her hair.*) I like women's hair. Why I washed and rolled and fixed my wife's hair all up when she died.
LACEY. Well, don't look at me. I'm not dead yet. Where're your tickets?
SAM. They're all gone.
LACEY. Well, excuse me but I believe I have t'go and powder my nose. (*Lacey gets up and walks over to Turnip, counting her tickets. To Turnip.*) Ring the bell sugar. I've already bled that fish dry. I gotta go reel in another one. (*Turnip looks at her coldly and then starts ringing the bell. He takes the record off. Music F stops. Cassidy goes over and sits next to Sam. He offers a stick of gum. Lacey runs over to Carmichael and Sue Jack. To Carmichael.*) Dance? Dance? Wanna dance? Wanna be mine?
CARMICHAEL. No thanks. (*He hands more tickets to Sue Jack. Music G — "Cryin' for the Carolines" — starts up.*)*
LACEY. I waltz, I foxtrot, I tango, I polka —
SUE JACK. Go ahead. I'm on break. (*Sue Jack hands a ticket to Lacey. Lacey grabs the ticket and pulls Carmichael tightly into her arms.*)
LACEY. Come on now. Who's your sugar? (*Sue Jack goes over to pour herself some coffee. Turnip comes up to her.*)
TURNIP. Boy oh boy.
SUE JACK. What?
TURNIP. Well, Hooker, he — he's gone and gotten himself back in love with you. Says he just can't help it. Says he never could.
SUE JACK. Look, I don't want him loving me. (*Turnip echoes.*) We're finished.
TURNIP. You're finished. I don't get it.
SUE JACK. Where'd he go?

---

*See Special Note on copyright page.

TURNIP. He's out back. (*Turnip motions to the side door. Sue Jack heads outside. As she goes she passes Lacey who is trying to French-kiss Carmichael.*)
LACEY. (*To Carmichael.*) Come on, sugar, it's not like I've got trench mouth. Although once I did transmit the pinkeye to a man. But that was way back in Alabama.
TURNIP. I swear, I pray I never fall in love. It seems like such a terrible thing. (*Sue Jack comes outside. Hooker is there looking at the sky. He turns and looks at her then turns back to stare at the sky.*)
HOOKER. It's pitch-black out. Not a star in the sky. Isn't that an incredible sight. (*A beat.*) Come here to me.
SUE JACK. We're bad luck for each other.
HOOKER. I don't care.
SUE JACK. I'm not right for you.
HOOKER. You are.
SUE JACK. Well, I'm not the one who's gonna have your kid, am I?
HOOKER. No, you're not.
SUE JACK. She is.
HOOKER. That's right. That's how that went down.
SUE JACK. Do the right thing for once in your lousy life.
HOOKER. You're the right thing.
SUE JACK. I'm the wrong thing.
HOOKER. You're the only goddamned thing.
SUE JACK. Listen, Reed, I — I got sick in prison. I can't have another kid. Not ever.
HOOKER. Doesn't matter. It's okay. We'll do okay.
SUE JACK. No, look at me. I've lost it. The bloom of youth. It's gone. It's over. I jazzed it all away. But her, she's good for you, this Cassidy, I want you to have her and the kid and this place —
HOOKER. (*Overlapping.*) This is bullshit, woman. Just bullshit 'cause I don't want a goddamn thing in this world but for you to come here to me. Not a goddamn thing —
SUE JACK. I can't Reed. I can't ever be with you —
HOOKER. What do you mean?
SUE JACK. It's over, Christ, just let it be. Let it be!
HOOKER. I'm not gonna let it be!
SUE JACK. Alright, you wanna know?! Ya gotta know.

HOOKER. (*Overlapping.*) Yeah, I wanna know! Yeah, I gotta know!
SUE JACK. You wanna know about Andy. You wanna know about our son? Well, it was my fault.
HOOKER. It was a miserable accident. Couldn't be helped. He pulled away to chase a hummingbird—
SUE JACK. Jesus Christ, don't you get it? There was no goddamn hummingbird. I went into a speak t'get a drink. I left him standing there on the proch. He ran off, a car hit him and I was sitting there in the bar, slinging back a shot of whiskey.
HOOKER. You said you held tight. You said he pulled away from you.
SUE JACK. I lied.
HOOKER. God Almighty. (*Sue Jack turns and goes back inside. Inside Turnip starts clanging the bell as Music G ends.*)
SUE JACK. Hey! Yo! Friends! Let's play some cards!
TURNIP. Cards! Well, hot damn! Hot damn!
LACEY. What fun! What fun!
SUE JACK. Whitt, you game?
CARMICHAEL. Why yes, ma'am, I'm plenty game.
SUE JACK. Good. Fortuitously, I seem t'have a deck of playing cards right here in my silver evening bag.
CARMICHAEL. Well, now, as chance would have it I've a round tucked right inside my breast pocket.
SUE JACK. My, my, but good fortune certainly does abound. (*Sue Jack slings off her lace gloves.*)
TURNIP. Well, alright! Alright! Yes, sir! Yes, sir! (*They both sit down at a table and begin to expertly shuffle their decks. The others crowd around them, murmuring with excitement and amazement. Hooker enters.*)
SUE JACK. So what do you say we make this a real quick gamble. Three games of cut. Best two outta three. Working with a his and her deck.
HOOKER. What's going on here?
SUE JACK. A friendly game of cards.
CARMICHAEL. A very friendly game. What're the stakes?
SUE JACK. If I win I want your three hundred and fifty-five dollar stake on the Lucky Spot. If you win, well, then we can finish off what we started over on Esplanade Avenue.

CARMICHAEL. Deal me in. I feel lucky.
HOOKER. What's this now, Miss Sue, you gonna sacrifice yourself t'save my waning, dying ass?
SUE JACK. I'm just paying off some debts. That's all Hooker. Just paying off some debts.
HOOKER. There's no way. You don't have a prayer.
SUE JACK. Look, I lost most of our stinking money playing the horses and dogs and roosters. As I remember, I was always pretty good with cards.
HOOKER. Yeah, well, just look at your goddamn hands. They're all torn up, for Christ's sake.
SUE JACK. (*Angrily.*) Oh leave me alone. Just leave me the fuck alone! Here, cut. (*Sue Jack shoves the cards over to Carmichael.*)
CARMICHAEL. No, no, no. Ladies first.
SUE JACK. Ah, a gentleman's game. (*She cuts the cards.*) Queen of hearts. (*She shoves the cards to Carmichael.*) Cut. (*Carmichael cuts the cards.*)
CARMICHAEL. Jack of spades. (*Cheers from the people watching the game.*)
TURNIP. (*To Carmichael.*) Better luck next time, ol' buddy.
LACEY. She's still got the touch.
CARMICHAEL. And I still feel lucky. Cut. (*Sue Jack cuts the deck.*)
SUE JACK. King of hearts. (*Turnip echoes.*)
CARMICHAEL. And I thought this was a game of chance.
SUE JACK. Cut. (*Carmichael cuts the deck.*)
CARMICHAEL. Hmm. King of spades.
SUE JACK. My, my my, a lot of court cards in this deck.
CARMICHAEL. Cut.
HOOKER. I'm not watching this. I have no part in this. You're on your own. (*Hooker goes and pours himself a drink.*)
SUE JACK. Yeah, that's where I belong. (*To Turnip.*) Here, spit on my hands for luck. (*Turnip spits on her hands. She rubs them together then cuts the cards.*) Five of clubs.
CASSIDY. Oh no.
TURNIP. Damn.
LACEY. Sweet Jesus. (*Carmichael cuts the deck.*)
CARMICHAEL. Ah me. What have we here? Ace of diamonds.

CASSIDY. She lost.
SUE JACK. Let's have another go. What d'ya say t'a round of Mexican Sweat?
CARMICHAEL. But, I've won the pot, haven't I? Don't wanna risk losing that.
SUE JACK. Well, then I guess tonight's just not my night.
CARMICHAEL. Please, my good fortune embarrasses me. Now why don't you get your coat? (*Sue Jack goes and gets her coat and evening bag.*)
CASSIDY. Where ya going?
SUE JACK. Oh, out jazzing around. Keep the party going till I get back. (*Carmichael escorts Sue Jack toward the front door. Hooker comes toward them.*)
HOOKER. Let her go, Carmichael. She stays here.
CARMICHAEL. You may own that one, but this one here's a free woman.
SUE JACK. Come on now, Reed. A bet's a bet.
HOOKER. I said get the hell away from her. (*Hooker jerks Sue Jack away and starts going toward Carmichael. Carmichael draws a pearl-handled pistol and aims it at Hooker. Everyone freezes.*)
CARMICHAEL. I don't think so. Unless maybe you want your face shot off.
SUE JACK. Alright now. Everything's fine. Let's just get outta here. (*Sue Jack and Carmichael head for the door. Carmichael keeps the gun aimed at everybody. They are almost out the door when Hooker grabs a chair to clobber Carmichael.*)
HOOKER. No, goddamnit! (*Carmichael quickly fires two shots. Both of them barely miss Hooker.*)
SUE JACK. Hooker! Jesus Christ!
HOOKER. Oh I'm fine. Just put my nerves a little on edge.
CARMICHAEL. Next time I shoot between the eyes.
HOOKER. Listen, Carmichael, I'll pay ya the three fifty-five she owes ya — we'll call it even.
CARMICHAEL. I don't believe you have it.
HOOKER. I do if I sell this place to you. You want it so damn bad. Here, I'll sign it over.
SUE JACK. Jesus, Hooker, don't be a goddamn idiot! (*Carmichael produces the contract.*)
HOOKER. You pay me three hundred and fifty-five dollars less than this price. How's that?

CARMICHAEL. I said the price would drop five hundred dollars an hour or fraction thereof. That means that this property is now valued at fifteen hundred dollars less than the price quoted on that contract. Add the three hundred fifty-five dollars Sue Jack sold herself for and that only leaves you about two hundred dollars.
SUE JACK. Forget it. Come on, Whitt. Let's go. (*Sue Jack tries to drag Carmichael out the door.*)
HOOKER. (*To Sue Jack.*) You're not going.
SUE JACK. Damn it t'hell! Just 'cause I go and make a fool outta myself doesn't mean you have to follow suit!
HOOKER. Screw it. I just won the place through freak luck. It ain't nothing t'me. (*Carmichael hands a pen to Hooker.*)
SUE JACK. Stop it! Just stop! Christ, two hundred dollars won't even be enough t'pay off your debts!
HOOKER. So what? This place is a joke. I'm sick of fooling with it. Here, Carmichael. Take the damn thing! (*Hooker signs the paper. Sue Jack rushes in and slams the paper down on the table.*)
SUE JACK. Look, this is nothing to me. He's just one guy, one night. Christ, Reed, don't you realize how many men, how many times —
HOOKER. (*Overlapping.*) Stop it! Don't!
SUE JACK. (*Running on.*) . . . How many nights there were just t'survive in that prison.
HOOKER. (*Overlapping.*) No more. Please.
SUE JACK. (*Running on.*) This?! This is nothing! Nothing!!
HOOKER. (*Overlapping.*) Shut up. You. Be still.
SUE JACK. (*Running on.*) Why, there were days I'd do three prison guards for a cup of dirty water. And once for a pair of shoes I was on my knees — I crawled on my knees —
HOOKER. (*Overlapping.*) Stop! No more! Please! Please! Please! (*Hooker grabs her face in his hands and shakes her with a desperate passion.*) I can't have it. No more. Please. (*Hooker holds Sue Jack tightly. She stares at him dumbstruck; tears stream down her face. Cassidy watches Sue Jack and Hooker, feeling the electric passion between the couple. She turns and runs up the stairs.*)
TURNIP. (*Reaching for her.*) Hey! Hey —
CASSIDY. (*Ripping off the rope ring.*) Let me be! Let me be —

(*Hooker grabs Sue Jack to him. She pulls away. Hooker then gets the contract and hands it to Carmichael.*)

HOOKER. There's the papers. Take them.

CARMICHAEL. Thank you.

SUE JACK. Damn, damn, damn! (*Sue Jack exits out the front door.*)

HOOKER. Goddamnit! Come back here. I'm not running after you.

SUE JACK. (*Offstage.*) I can't, Reed. It's no good. Let it go. Please, let it go.

HOOKER. (*Overlapping.*) I'm not running after you! You hear me? Sue Jack! (*A beat. He runs out the front door after her. Offstage.*) Sue Jack! (*Hooker reenters.*) Hell. (*He slams out the kitchen door.*)

CARMICHAEL. (*To Turnip.*) Here's a check. Give it to him, will you?

TURNIP. Yeah.

CARMICHAEL. Oh, and please arrange to be out of here by January one. That's when the drilling crew — oh well, those high finance matters don't really concern you, poor people, now do they? Well, good night, everyone.

LACEY. Look, Mr. Carmichael —

CARMICHAEL. What?

LACEY. Don't go away lonesome. I'll keep ya company for the night.

CARMICHAEL. Well, it's funny. I've always liked blondes but I'm going to make an exception in your case. Good night now. (*Carmichael exits out the front door.*)

LACEY. Well, he certainly is a spoilsport, isn't he? A man like that doesn't do anybody any good. He's too prissy. Thinks just 'cause he's rich nobody but him matters in the whole wide world. (*She falls and trips.*) Oh, my poor ankle. (*To Turnip.*) Help me up, will you, sugar?

TURNIP. Are you sure your ankles are really weak?

LACEY. What?

TURNIP. Maybe you just pretend they're weak. Maybe you just like t'fall down.

LACEY. Don't be stupid. Nobody likes t'fall down.

TURNIP. No, you're wrong. A lot of people like t'fall down. And why not? It's easy. Ya just go right with the pull of things. Right with the flow. Ya don't ever gotta worry about standing on your own two feet. The only tough part is dragging yourself back up again. Getting back up. (*A beat.*) Yeah, that can be a lot of work.

LACEY. Then help me up. Please.

TURNIP. Help your own self up. (*Lacey drags herself to her feet.*)

LACEY. Oooh! (*Hooker walks in from the kitchen carrying a jug of moonshine. He takes a slug. Lacey turns and looks at him.*) Oooh! I just don't understand, people always despise me, no matter where I go! (*Lacey exits out the side door and disappears through the yard.*)

HOOKER. Women. Christ, they're all the same.

TURNIP. Sweet Jesus. Nobody's got any sense in this world; nobody. We just let it all slip right on past us. No wonder why we keep coming up empty-handed. No damn wonder. (*Turnip exits out the kitchen door. Hooker pauses a beat then turns to Sam.*)

HOOKER. Well, looks like I spoiled everybody's Christmas Eve. So, you having a good time?

SAM. Oh yeah.

HOOKER. Good. I'll put on some more music. (*Hooker puts on Music H — "Sweet Lorraine."* The music plays.*) Want some punch? We got cookies.

SAM. I'm, well, I'm outta tickets.

HOOKER. Forget about it. It's all on the house. Everything's all on the house. (*Hooker tosses Sam a cookie. The two men sway to the music a moment.*) Pretty tune. (*The music swells and the lights fade to blackout.*)

END OF SCENE 2

ACT II

Scene 3

The setting is the same. Cassidy sits at a table humming as she makes paper hats out of newspaper. She wears a

---

*See Special Note on copyright page.

simple dress and has a bow in her hair. The coffee pot is out on the counter. It is sunrise.
Lacey sits on a stump in the outside area. She wears her tattered robe.
Sue Jack comes in the front door. She wears the same dress she had on the night before. She carries a branch of holly.

CASSIDY. Good morning.
SUE JACK. 'Morning.
CASSIDY. It's a pretty morning.
SUE JACK. (*Undecided.*) Yeah.
CASSIDY. You alright?
SUE JACK. I—no.
CASSIDY. Well, I reckon I outta tell ya I broken off my marriage t' Hooker. Tore off the engagement ring. It's gone.
SUE JACK. Well, look, ya better forget about all that and make it up with him. It'll be alright. You'll just make it up.
CASSIDY. Ain't nothing t'make up. The thing is I can't never awaken no love in him for me—'cause, well, he's got you in his blood; you're his partner.
SUE JACK. I sure as hell don't know about that.
CASSIDY. I do. See I ain't stupid. I know people getting married's supposed to be in love with the people they's getting married to. Ya don't want somebody just marrying ya on the rebound. And it's funny but it makes me feel lighthearted, 'cause now I see, well, maybe love ain't a made-up lie like Santa Claus or something. Maybe it can be true. And if it's true, maybe I can find someone I'd shoot off guns for and find someone who'll hold my face and tell me, please, please, please. Or maybe he'll just, I don't know, give me a slice of watermelon and pick out all the seeds. Why, having this child don't even scare me no more. 'Cause if ya have this love inside ya it don't matter if your father was a lord in a castle or a bum on the road or a murderer in a cage. It don't matter. Well, here's a hat for ya. Merry Christmas. (*Cassidy puts a paper hat on Sue Jack's head. Turnip enters from* R. *He carries a branch of mistletoe. He spots Lacey.*)
LACEY. Hi.
TURNIP. Hi. (*Turnip passes her and heads for the side door.*)

LACEY. I guess you think I'm just a gold digger. Well, maybe I am. But if I am it's cause I went broke trying t'crash the movies and all my stuff's in pawn and I don't even have a decent rag on my back. Gosh, the main thing I wanted outta life was fame, wealth and adoration. Instead I'm poor and broke and nobody likes me.
TURNIP. I like talking t'ya. Ya seemed interested in what I had t'say.
LACEY. Really?
TURNIP. Yeah.
LACEY. Oh my, my, my! (*Lacey staggers around in a dither. Suddenly she realizes she is about to fall and quickly sits back down on the stump.*) How nice. Thank you very much, Turnip.
TURNIP. Tell me . . .
LACEY. Yes?!
TURNIP. Do you think I should change my name from Turnip t'something else? I mean, so people — so girls would like me better.
LACEY. Hmm. Well, ya know what they say, "A turnip by any other name would smell as sweet."
TURNIP. Never thought of it like that. Wanna go inside?
LACEY. Sure. (*Lacey stands up and they move from the outside area to the ballroom through the side door.*) Merry Christmas, everyone!
SUE JACK & CASSIDY. Merry Christmas.
LACEY. Look, I've brought over my spray bottle of genuine French perfume. As a gift I'm allowing everyone four sprays apiece. (*To Sue Jack.*) Here, sugar, you go first.
SUE JACK. Well, thanks, Lacey.
TURNIP. (*To Cassidy.*) Here, I brought ya some mistletoe.
SUE JACK. Mmm. Smells good.
TURNIP. If ya put it over two people's heads, they gotta kiss underneath it. (*He holds the mistletoe over their heads.*) See, like this. (*He kisses her.*) It's part of Christmas. (*He hands out the mistletoe to her.*)
CASSIDY. (*Taking it from him.*) Thanks. (*Cassidy goes solemnly up to Sue Jack.*) Oh look, you're under mistletoe. Kiss me quick. (*They kiss. Cassidy walks over to Lacey.*) Now you're under mistletoe. Kiss me. It's part of Christmas. (*They kiss. Cassidy turns and says to Turnip.*) What a fun gift. (*She holds the*

mistletoe over his head and they kiss again. Hooker and Sam enter the outdoor area. Hooker carries a sack of oranges. Sam carries some peppermint candy canes. Hooker still wears his evening clothes.)

HOOKER. How many sugar candies ya got?

SAM. 'Bout a dozen.

HOOKER. Well, that oughta be plenty. I'll eat one now. (*Hooker takes a candy cane, sits down on the bench and starts eating it.*)

SAM. Ain't we going in?

HOOKER. You go on in. I don't figure I'm gonna get such a heartwarming reception.

SAM. Well, alright. And thanks for having me over for Christmas. I didn't have no other place t'go.

HOOKER. No, me neither. (*Sam knocks on the side door and says "Hello." Everyone welcomes him.*)

LACEY. Well, look who's here!

CASSIDY. Sam, come on in.

TURNIP. Hey, Merry Christmas.

SAM. Thanks. I hope ya don't mind me coming unexpected.

CASSIDY. Oh, no.

SAM. Hooker, he's the one asked me.

SUE JACK. Where is he anyway?

SAM. Just sitting out back. I brought y'all some sugar candies. (*Sam hands out the candy. Sue Jack heads for the side door.*)

LACEY. Oh look! Sweets! Sugar sweets!

CASSIDY. Why, thanks, Sam.

TURNIP. Thanks. (*Sue Jack stands at the side door watching Hooker eat his candy cane on the bench.*)

SUE JACK. Hi.

HOOKER. Hi. You're back.

SUE JACK. Yeah. Just now. I was out walking. And thinking. Did a lot of thinking.

HOOKER. What'd ya think?

SUE JACK. That I miss you. A lot. A real lot.

HOOKER. Yeah, well, sorry t'say — I miss you too.

SUE JACK. Ya do? Well, thanks. I appreciate it. God I — thanks.

HOOKER. Oh don't be so damn grateful. It makes me feel like an idiot.

SUE JACK. Sorry.
HOOKER. Forget it.
SUE JACK. Sure. I guess I don't really know how to be. I mean there's so much water under the bridge. So much muddy, muddy goddamn water.
HOOKER. Yeah, yeah. I know, I know. So do us both a favor and let's not wallow in it.
SUE JACK. We don't wanna wallow in it.
HOOKER. That reminds me. Our hog's gone. The Christmas pig. Somebody stole it. I don't know what t'do. You got any ideas?
SUE JACK. Well . . . let's see now. I passed by a pumpkin patch this morning. I could go borrow three or four and make us up some pumpkin pudding.
HOOKER. That'd be a treat. We haven't had that in, well, years.
SUE JACK. Yeah. It's been years. Hope I remember how t'make it.
HOOKER. Well, don't ya put a nickel in it?
SUE JACK. Right. Whoever finds the nickel in their portion will have a stroke of dumb luck.
HOOKER. Well, we sure could use some dumb luck.
SUE JACK. We sure could.
HOOKER. God Almighty. T'dumb luck. (*He reaches into the air, and a nickel appears in his fingers. He hands the nickel to Sue Jack.*)
SUE JACK. T'dumb luck. (*They both start to laugh.*)
HOOKER. Now, Christ, will ya come here, please! (*They go into each other's arms.*)
SUE JACK. (*After a beat.*) Merry Christmas, Reed.
HOOKER. Merry Christmas to you, sweet Sue. (*They kiss passionately. (Inside Cassidy sits on top of a table. She wears a paper hat and waves a candy cane.*)
CASSIDY. Once I had my fortune told and the fortune-teller tol' me I had a future right here in the palm of my hand. Why this could be the beginning of my future. This could be it! (*Music I — "Sunny Side of the Street"* — starts to*

---

*See Special Note on copyright page.

play on the record player. Sue Jack and Hooker enter from the side door.)
HOOKER. Merry Christmas, everyone! Merry Christmas!
ALL. (*To Hooker.*) Merry Christmas!
HOOKER. Here're some oranges for ya. (*Hooker starts throwing oranges to everyone from his sack.*)
TURNIP. Oranges, look! Oranges!
LACEY. I love citrus!
CASSIDY. They're beautiful!
HOOKER. Yeah, they are. Hey, I wanna dance! I wanna dance with every one of ya! It's Christmas morning and I wanna dance with everyone. (*Everyone starts dancing. They all keep changing partners. Men dance with women, men dance with men, women dance with women. People dance alone. Everyone dances with everyone else as the lights slowly fade to blackout and the music continues to play.*)

END OF PLAY

PROPERTY LIST

TOP OF SHOW
Carousel horse that spins
Old wood stump
Leafless tree
U.L. Porch:
   Piano
   Ice cream chairs (3)
   Folding chairs (4)
   Tables (2)
Counter Door:
   Ties on cane
   (3 including Sam's tie looped together)
Mantel:
   Dressing bottles with colored water
   Breakaway bottle
   Unbroken mirror
Sign and ladder: U. of mantel
Bucket with hot water and rag on crate: D. of mantel
Stove with coffee pot: D.L.
L. plug: unplugged
Bar facing up
Bar Shelf:
   Shot glasses (4), (1) double (wash)
   Whiskey (Coke and water)
   White liquor
   White Mule in Mason jar (change)
   Towel
   Cigar box (empty)
   Sewing tin with (2) spools thread
      1 needle threaded
      1 needle on spool
Nails (2)
Knife
Empty bottle
Top of stairs: metal tray

U. Closet:
   Broom
   Hammer
   Keg
   Boards (2)
   Toolbox (closed)
Spittoon: D. Bar
Tall stool: U.
Short stool: D.
Jukebox: rigged
Felt Table: L. of jukebox
   Deck of cards
   Metal chair
Cassidy's sweater:
   D. end o'bar
   (birthday note in pocket)
Pine needles: L.C.

OFF LEFT

ACT I
Oatmeal carton, carpenter's pencil
Skillet with breakfast
Fork, knife, cup
Sue Jack's purse with gifts
(snowman mittens, felt bell)
Hooker's shirt
Grey bucket/cranberries
Basin/popcorn/needle and thread

ACT II

Paper hats (5)
Flour sack with pillow
Moonshine jug (water)
Shot glass
Holly branch

FOR HALF TIME
Village/strike to silo
Battery generator
Broken record for jukebox

Record player
Records on crate with albums
Bells (2)
Punch bowl/water
Plate/cookies
Hooker's top hat
Tickets (62)
Streamers (17)
Paper tree chain
Coffee pot in silo

OFF RIGHT

ACT I
Bare tree
Saw
Comb
Dress (Cassidy/Act II)
Sue Jack's box:
    bear, red shoes (black gloves, rouge), cards, hand lotion, silver mirror, evening bag (stacked cards), orange coat, pink hat, fabric

ACT II
Perfume atomizer
Mistletoe
Bag of oranges
White paper cone/(12) candy canes – (9) fake, (3) real
Dressed tree (for half time)
Bucket of pine needles

DRESSING ROOM
Sue Jack: Coat with string in pocket
Cassidy: Yellow string engagement ring
           Birthday note in sweater pocket
Lacey: Blue purse with eye pencil, lipstick, compact
           Strike tickets
Turnip: Mug on string (wash)
Reed: Cup of blood
           Nails (2)
           Plastic nickel
Whitt: Flask/water

　　　　　　　Gun/loaded
　　　　　　　Stacked cards (bicycle deck)
　　　　　　　Checkbook
　　　　　　　Fountain pen/ink
　　　　　　　Powder
　　　　　　　Briefcase (stuffed)/sheriff's order
　　　　　　　Contract
　　　　　　　Wallet/money
　　　　　　　Fake dime
　　　　　　　Blood
　　　　　　　Cigarettes
Sam:　　　　Quarters (2)
　　　　　　　Dimes (7)
　　　　　　　Gum

HALF TIME
Switch trees (plug in)
Add village (plug in)
Add generator
Change mirror
Put up bar facing
Broken record on jukebox
Add hot water to coffee pot
On Bar:
　　Record player, on, open, with record, needle on
　　Bells (2)
　　Punch bowl with water
　　Plate with cookies
Shelf 1:
　　Sue Jack's evening bag with loaded cards, black gloves
　　Shot glasses
　　Hammer
　　Act I stuff
Shelf 2: Megaphone
D. of Bar:
　　Record crate with records
　　Spittoon
Hooker's top hat: D. end of mantel
Stairs:
　　Cigar box

Ticket roll
Strike ladder
Add mirror ball
Cane with ties to porch
Strike Sue Jack's box to L.
Strike pink fabric from box
Reed's jacket to U. closet
Reset Bar stools
Clean up water and popcorn
Close doors
Tape up signs
Close toolbox
Streamers:
   mantel (4)
   bar velcro (2)
   stairs (2)
   porch area (7)
   U.L. door (2)
Paper chain on tree

COSTUME PLOT

CASSIDY SMITH
ACT I
Under all costumes — pregnancy padding built on leotard — 8 months
Grey and white checked cotton 20's style dress, "distressed"
"Dirty" short sleeved union suit
Black and white flecked cardigan sweater
Beat up grey derby
High top brown leather work boots
   Tries on Sue Jack's hat, coat, shoes — worn in Act II, 1 & 2

ACT II, Scene 1
Orange silk 20's party dress — sleeveless — with handkerchief hem and self-fabric flowers down center front ruching
Orange silk velvet evening coat with hood and slight train — trimmed with brown mink at hood — very "distressed"
Pink satin and gold lace cloche hat with small brim and "berry" trim
Red silk shoes with strap across instep

ACT II, Scene 2
Same

ACT II, Scene 3
Return to dress, union suit and shoes of Act I without derby and sweater

LACEY ROLLINS
ACT I
Pale pink silk 20's teddy
Cerise, orange and gold voided velvet 20's style wrapper with orange ostrich feather trim
Pansy print and lavendar leather high heel shoes with ankle straps
Crystal drop earrings

ACT II, Scene 1
20's style party dress with dropped waist — in "worn" green velvet bodice; skirt made of 3 flounces of pink net with gold metallic polka dots
Rhinestone drop earrings
Rhinestone necklace with green stone in center
Cerise silk stockings with runs
Small royal blue silk embroidered evening bag "distressed"
Repeat shoes

ACT II, Scene 2
Same

ACT II, Scene 3
Return to Act I costume

SUE JACK TILLER HOOKER
ACT I
Beige tweed 20's coat — too small
Purple crocheted lace scarf on head
Gold and blue print cotton 20's style dress with short sleeves and buttons down center front — too large
Dipped down long underwear
Dipped down cotton ankle socks
Black and white woven handbag on wooden frame
Fake lizard oxford style shoes with low heels
    Adds from box of old belongings: black crocheted lace gloves

ACT II, Scene 1
Cerise silk satin 20's style evening dress with handkerchief hem; with rhinestone straps and dangling rhinestone trim at cow neckline
Rhinestone drop earrings
Clear and white beaded evening bag
Gold glitter open-toed high heel shoes with straps across instep
Coat from Act I over

ACT II, Scene 2
Same — without coat —
Add black lace crocheted gloves

ACT II, Scene 3
Same

TURNIP MOSS
ACT I
"Distressed" athletic shirt
Brown and grey plaid collarless shirt — too small
Brown overalls — "distressed"
Black high-top work boots — "distressed"

ACT II, Scene 1
Add brown knit vest

ACT II, Scene 2
Add tan tweed Norfolk jacket
Add red tie

ACT II, Scene 3
Remove vest, jacket, tie
Add coonskin cap

REED HOOKER
ACT I
White shirt — torn and bloody
Faded grey cotton work handkerchief over wound
Black wool formal trousers with suspenders — "distressed"
Green velvet evening jacket — "distressed"
Brown wing-tip shoes — "distressed"
   Change to: clean shirt — blue and white stripe, collarless with rip
   Duplicate shirt — more "distressed" and bloody

ACT II, Scene 1
Keep trousers and shoes
Wing collar formal shirt with studs and cuff links
White pique formac vest
Black silk tie

ACT II, Scene 2
Add — tattered tailcoat — *not* a match with trousers
Slightly battered black silk collapsible top hat

ACT II, Scene 3
Remove tailcoat and hat

WHITT CARMICHAEL
ACT I
Royal blue double-breasted suit (with suspenders)
White dress shirt with navy monograms and jenelled cuff links
Deep red silk tie, pocket handkerchief and fleur-de-lys tie pin
Navy blue felt fedora
Black and white spectator shoes
(2) Rings — flashy

ACT II, Scene 2
Add — white silk scarf
Navy blue cashmere overcoat with brown fur collar

SAM
ACT II Scene 2
Blue and white shirt with small collar
Well-worn but clean denim overalls
Well-worn denim work jacket
High top brown leather work boots — "distressed"
Grey felt fedora — "distressed"

ACT II, Scene 3
Repeat

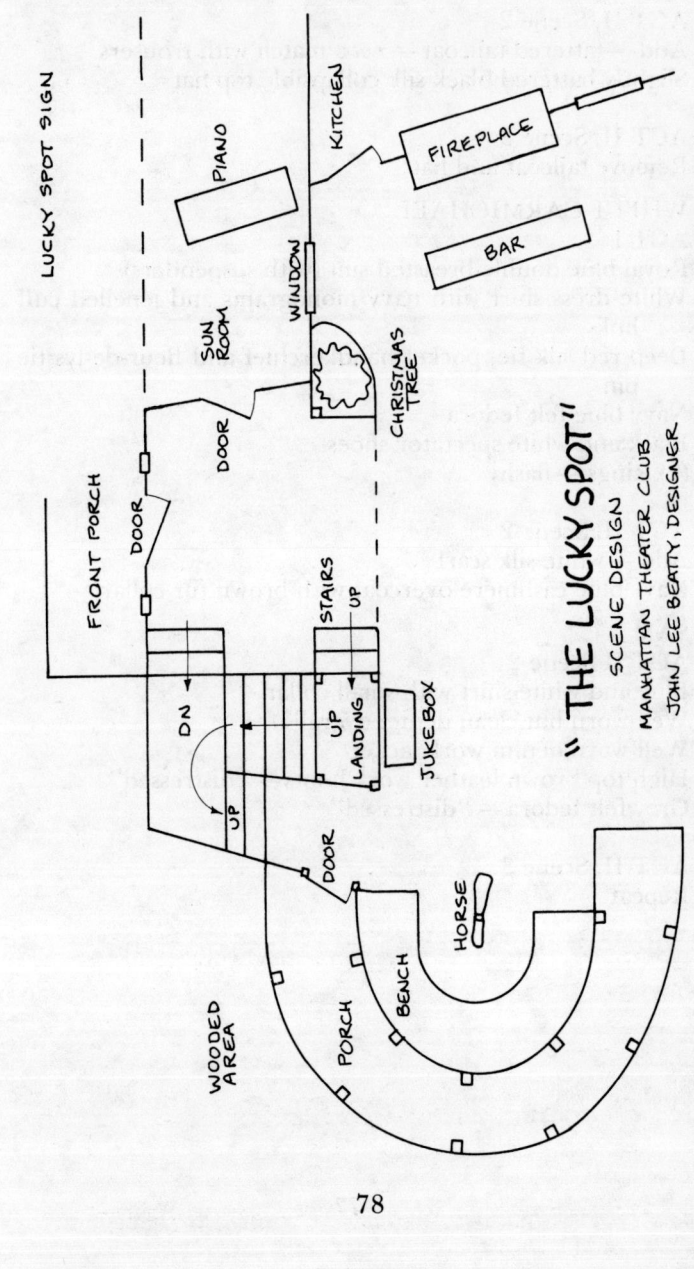

New PLAYS

SWEET SUE
THE COMMON PURSUIT
ELEEMOSYNARY
AMERICAN DREAMS
BOUNCERS
PHAEDRA
THE MADERATI
LILY DALE
RUNNING ON EMPTY
T BONE N WEASEL
MRS. CALIFORNIA
FUN & NOBODY
MAN DANGLING
THE WIDOW CLAIRE

Inquiries Invited

DRAMATISTS PLAY SERVICE, INC.
440 Park Avenue South New York, N. Y. 10016

NEW Plays

STEEL MAGNOLIAS
THE LUCKY SPOT
THE DREAMER EXAMINES HIS PILLOW
BODIES, REST, AND MOTION
HOW TO SAY GOODBYE
JACOB'S LADDER
PASTA
MR. 80%
TRACERS
DANGER: MEMORY!
VANISHING ACT
PROGRESS
THE DREAM COAST
JITTERS

DRAMATISTS PLAY SERVICE, INC.
440 PARK AVENUE SOUTH   NEW YORK, N.Y. 10016